WITH MY REGIMENT

Published by

The Naval & Military Press Ltd
Unit 5 Riverside, Brambleside
Bellbrook Industrial Estate
Uckfield, East Sussex
TN22 1QQ England

Tel: +44 (0)1825 749494

www.naval-military-press.com
www.nmarchive.com

*In reprinting in facsimile from the original, any imperfections are inevitably reproduced
and the quality may fall short of modern type and cartographic standards.*

WITH MY REGIMENT
FROM THE AISNE TO LA BASSÉE

BY
"PLATOON COMMANDER"

The Naval & Military Press Ltd

TO "PAT"

*Who was killed in front of La Bassée on
October 21, 1914, this book is
affectionately dedicated
by the author*

ACKNOWLEDGMENT

The author desires to thank the Editors of The English Review, The Evening Standard, *and* The Westminster Gazette *for kind permission to reproduce in this volume, articles which appeared in their various columns.*

CONTENTS

CHAP.	PAGE
INTRODUCTION	1
I. TAKING OUT A DRAFT	8
II. RAILHEAD AND BEYOND	25
III. EARLY DAYS ON THE AISNE	40
IV. IN BILLETS	58
V. THE MOVE UP (1)	71
VI. THE MOVE UP (2)	83
VII. NEARING THE FIRING-LINE	93
VIII. GETTING INTO ACTION	101
IX. AN ATTACK AT DAWN	111
X. THE RESERVE COMPANY	120
XI. A NIGHT ATTACK	129
XII. THE FARM IN THE FIRING-LINE	138
XIII. PUSHING FORWARD	146
XIV. IN FRONT OF LA BASSÉE	156

CONTENTS

CHAP.		PAGE
XV.	A NIGHT PATROL	166
XVI.	WITH THE SUPPORTS	176
XVII.	BETWEEN ACTIONS	187
XVIII.	"THE ——TH BRIGADE WILL ATTACK ——"	197
XIX.	BY THE SKIN OF OUR TEETH	206
XX.	"AND THENCE TO BED"	220

INTRODUCTION

"REPORT yourself to O.C. 1st Battalion at —— immediately.—GROUP."

So the time had come. Of course I guessed what was going to be in the wire before I opened it, but somehow the pink telegraph envelope, and that little word Group at the end of the message, shook me out of an exciting day-dream into reality. For years we had been brought up on the word "GROUP," which was to come at the end of the order for mobilization. Now it was being flashed over wires all over the country. Our training was to bear fruit. The happy, careless—some people say, rather useless—life of the army officer in peace time was over. The country had gone to war.

I was staying at the time in a large house by the banks of the Thames. My hostess was a mother of soldiers. She took the news calmly, as a mother of soldiers should; said good-bye to her eldest boy, who was to go with the first troops that left England, arranged for the outfit of her two second sons, and sent for her baby from Eton, whom she saw dispatched to the Royal Military College. It was a great house to be in on the outbreak of war—a house whose sons to the third and fourth generation had built up the British Empire, and which, now, when the Empire was called upon to fight for its life, stood firm and undismayed.

I went up to London to my rooms to collect a few things. My landlady was breathless with helping me pack, aghast at the National crisis, and rather shocked at my levity. Levity— yes, I suppose I was flippant. What else could one be when suddenly told one was going to war with Germany ? I was rather enjoying the packing and everything up to a point, but as I ransacked drawers I came on a bundle of letters with some absurd comic postcards. The letters had a faint scent of violet about them. They had to be sealed up and left behind, with directions for their disposal if I didn't come back. And there was a photograph to be taken from the mantelpiece and put in a pocket-book, a photograph which had been in many places with me. Well, now it must go on its travels again. I got an aching in the back of my throat and hurried to my club for a drink.

From the club I went to the station. There was a big crowd on the platform of the boat-train. Many women had come to see their menfolk off, and some to travel with them as far as they could. There were also a great many people who were crossing over to Ireland under the impression that it would be the last night of the Channel service for civilian traffic. There were business men, and people whose homes were in Ireland, and officials. All looked a little anxious, as much as to say, "Well, it has begun!"

Our journey was uneventful until we came alongside the wharf at ——, and here newsboys met us with placards, "ENGLAND DECLARES WAR ON GERMANY."

At the camp I reported myself to the Adjutant. There was little in his manner to show that he was getting a regiment ready to go to war, except that he showed an indisposition to talk, and seemed trying to keep his mind clear of everything except for the sequence of things which had to be done.

After reporting to the Adjutant I went

across to the mess. The mess was in a state of packing. Cases, boxes, and litter of all descriptions blocked the corridors; each officer's room was like the interior of a furniture removal van, and the mess waiters were busy packing away all the regimental silver and pictures. The only things which stood out clearly from the jumble were the field-service kits of the different officers.

These were for the most part all neatly rolled up in brown or green valises ready to be thrown on the transport wagon at an instant's notice. Now and again an officer would come to a pair of scales outside the mess, weigh his kit, and then start frantically to undo it, pull out a pair of boots or a blanket, and roll it up again. It took some nice adjustment to get all that was wanted into the 35 lb. allowed.

The following morning we heard a band and cheering, and looking out of the window saw some three hundred men marching up from the station. All the regiment turned out to greet the new arrivals—they were fine men in the prime of life, and swung along evidently well used to pack and rifle. They were the

INTRODUCTION

old soldiers of the regiment—reservists who had been called back to the Colours on mobilization from civil life.

They had been down to the depot, thrown off their civilian clothes, and taken up their rifles once more. They had most of them served under many of the officers who were still with the regiment. It put heart into all, and strengthened the general feeling of confidence that we should see the thing through, to see so many old faces coming back to march with the regiment once more.

For a night or two before the regiment embarked we dined in mess thirty strong. I used to wonder, as we sat round the table, looking at the faces of my brother officers, what fate held in store for them, how many would come back, how others would die. It was going to be " a hell of a war." All were agreed on that. There was no feeling of going off for a day's hunting about anyone. Men made their wills quietly, packed their belongings, and wrote letters of good-bye to their friends.

One grey morning at six the regiment marched across the open plain behind the barracks to the little siding. A few officers' wives and those left behind came to see them off, but there was no cheering and few tears. The train stole quietly out of the station, and the regiment went to war.

"Well—see you out soon," Goyle called to me.

"Yes—I expect so," I answered, and said good-bye to him and the others.

Alas, there are few left now to read these words. The war continues. Of the survivors a half have still to serve. For me, my fighting days are done. I am not sorry. Whatever ideas I had as a cadet, this war has taught me that fighting is too fierce and heart-racking to be a sport or anything except a duty.

These sketches of war as I saw it I write once more by the banks of the upper reaches of the Thames, calm and beautiful with her fringe of browning leaves, as she was stately and magnificent in full midsummer a year before. Now autumn has come and the dead leaves lie in the golden sunlight.

Of my brother officers, who read these words, I ask only the kindly tolerance they have always shown. Should they recognize themselves in deeds described, and find fault with the accuracy of the account, will they remember that it is difficult to give chapter and verse without notes to refer to. And for notes, I think all will agree that to have taken them for such a purpose while out there would have been a waste of time.

"PLATOON COMMANDER."

I. TAKING OUT A DRAFT

I WAS sitting drinking a gin-and-bitters in the lounge of the big hotel facing the sea when Mulligan came dashing in.

"I say, you're wanted back at the barracks at once. You've got to come out with me with the draft to-night."

"All right, old son, have a gin-and-bitters anyway. What time does the train start?"

"In an hour's time—seven o'clock," said Mulligan, still much excited, but not, however, making any attempt to move away as the waiter approached.

"Well, here's to the enterprise and our handsome selves," he said a few minutes later, raising his glass.

Mulligan was not handsome; he had a face the colour of boiled beetroot, very blue eyes, and a humorous mouth. He was a Special Reserve subaltern, who before the war had done a chequered month's training with the battalion every year, and spent the other eleven months interesting himself in aviation,

TAKING OUT A DRAFT 9

theatrical life, and the motor business. To go out to the Front with him as one's colleague in charge of a draft of 180 men was a certain way of avoiding *ennui*.

We had been waiting some while with the reserve battalion for our turn to go out, and now, just four weeks after the regiment sailed with the vanguard of the Expeditionary Force, we were sent for at two hours' notice.

We were ready, of course. There was not much to get ready, except our 35 lb. kit, and that we always kept rolled up by our beds. Our revolvers, field-glasses, water-bottles, and haversacks were hung on our belts, and we had only to tell our servants to take our kits down to the transport wagon and walk on to the square where the draft was paraded, which we did.

The Colonel said a few words, the town band fell in at the head of the column, the crowd waved good-bye, and the draft cheered and yelled and sang their way to the station. The draft was in the best of spirits; it cheered the colonel, adjutant, and any officers on sight; it leant out of the carriage windows and waved beer bottles, and rifles, and caps; and it greeted with such uproarious applause any attempt to give orders on the part of Mulligan or myself that we thought it best to remain in the corner of our first-class carriage. There were 180 men of all ages from nineteen to forty, old soldiers and young soldiers, militiamen, reservists, and a few regulars.

"We are going to have a jolly time with these," said Mulligan, indicating the draft.

Our transport was a converted Blue Line boat, which the trip before had brought over German prisoners, and the trip before that cattle from America. She had been carpentered up to carry troops, and her hold was a network of planks and scaffolding. She was to carry, besides ourselves, drafts for five other regiments, and each of these had to receive, on embarkation, rations to last for five days.

From the moment we got on board Mulligan began to prove invaluable. He collected our full number of rations from the bewildered and suspicious Army Service Corps official, he annexed an easily defended corner in the hold, stored the rations there, and put a guard over them; he frightened two other draft officers out of the only remaining officer's cabin and

TAKING OUT A DRAFT

put our kit on to their bunks, and finally, when all was quiet, he led me to a hotel in the port where we could get a drink after ten.

The transport sailed the next morning, and once under way there was little or nothing for officers and men to do except lie about in the sun. It was a glorious September morning as we steamed past the Isle of Wight, with only two destroyers, one ahead and one to port, to remind us we were at war. But as we sat smoking and talking on deck there was a feeling in the air which dispelled the sense of being on a pleasure trip.

I think that just for those few hours as we left the shores of England there was heaviness in each man's heart. It was no holiday this we were going on. There was an officer in a Highland regiment, who was one of fifteen officers of the same regiment on their way out to replace fifteen brother officers who had only crossed the sea four weeks before: a splendid-looking fellow, with his kilt and gaily cocked glengarry; there would be very few fellows in the regiment that he knew out there now, he said to me. He had rather a serious expression. It was grim work going out to fill the place of a friend who had been killed. And there was another fellow whom I'd known well years ago and who welcomed me with delight when he found we were to be on the same transport. "You know, I don't like this a bit," he said, evidently much relieved to find some one to whom he could speak his heart, instead of keeping up the conventional mask of joy at having been ordered to the Front. "As far as I can see, one is certain to be killed."

We talked over old days when we had been quartered near London and gone off together to Covent Garden balls and other entertainments. "You know, I'm married now," he told me. "You're *not?*" I said, laughing; it seems so funny when one's bachelor friends get married; and he looked just the same dog as ever.

"Yes, I've been married a year—got a brat too," he said with an air of having conclusively reformed; then, returning to the subject of the war, "absolutely certain to get hit, you know—it's all very well—never even had time to say good-bye to my wife and kid."

A month or two afterwards I saw from the

TAKING OUT A DRAFT 13

papers that his regiment had been in action and lost fourteen officers—eleven wounded and three killed. It seemed just the infernal luck of the thing that he should have been one of the three killed.

The voyage lasted three days. By the middle of the second day quite half the troops were sea-sick. It also came on to rain. The men had therefore all to remain in the hold. Owing to the exigencies of war they had to be packed like Chinese coolies, and there was no room for them to walk about, barely enough for them to lie down. The boards on which they lay soon became littered with bits of biscuit, cheese, clots of jam, and fragments of bully beef. The rain found its way down to the hold through the improvised companion ways, and not more than half the men could keep dry. The stench in the hold soon became appalling. The men themselves did not seem to worry much, but lay about, those who were well enough smoking, those who were not, with the aggrieved expression Tommy often wears when he is sorely tried, as much as to say : " —— it, what next am I going to be asked to do ? " But when Tommy wears this expression it by no means follows he is not going to carry out the command. He retreated from Mons in this fashion.

The sun was shining again as we arrived off the mouth of the Loire. As we steamed slowly up the river we began to see the first signs of war. There was a large concentration camp on the left bank. We were passed and were vociferously cheered by another transport, lying off the dock with her decks thick with men waiting to be disembarked. We were eventually moored alongside a quay and told we must all remain on board till to-morrow morning. This was a disappointment to the men, a few of whom endeavoured to land on their own initiative by means of a rope ladder. A guard was put over the ladder and most of the officers retired to the saloon for drinks. We had various distractions during the evening. First a visit from a wounded officer who had been sent down from the base camp. He said his regiment had been badly cut up. Some of the others asked him about individual officers in his regiment. "The colonel—oh, the colonel has 'gone.' Chippendale—poor Chippendale, he thought he'd been hit in the

TAKING OUT A DRAFT 15

stomach and was dead. 'Curtes,' yes, Curtes had been alongside him in the trench and shot through the head. There was a fellow in hospital with him who had had eleven bullets in his leg. He was dying. He didn't know how long he'd be at the base camp. They had tried to put him on a hospital boat for England, but he had got off again. He thought he'd go back in a week. It was awful up there."

He was the first wounded man we had seen, and we said one to another: "By Jove, he has been through it."

Now I know that his funny way of saying everybody was dead, and the shocked look on his face, combined with the wish to go back, and "we are in for a bigger thing than we ever thought" attitude, were all symptoms of nervous strain, which most men get after a certain time in action.

Besides our visitor we saw something of the life of the town from the sides of the boat. There were a good many men in khaki coming and going along the streets and in cafés, apparently all rather the worse for drink, and there was an officer's picket parading the streets putting the more drunken under arrest. It was the first few days of the new base camp, and the provost-marshal was just getting the town in order.

As Mulligan and I were turning in for the night an orderly reported that a man had been drowned trying to get off the boat, and an officer was wanted to go down to the quay. Mulligan was up immediately. It seemed rather an unpleasant job for a boy like him, so I said there was no need for him to go as the man might not belong to our draft.

He grinned and put on his cap. " I think I'll go and get a sight of my first corpse," he said.

It was pouring with rain when we landed the next morning. We were told to march to No. 7a base camp, which we should find two miles outside the town, shown the direction, and off we started. There were the details of some five divisions quartered round the town, first reinforcements, second reinforcements, artillery units, cavalry, A.S.C., and Royal Flying Corps. As these were all divided into various small settlements, which each guarded its domain jealously and denied

TAKING OUT A DRAFT 17

all knowledge of us when we offered ourselves for accommodation, it was no easy matter to arrive at the right spot. It rained steadily during our search; however, at last, after plodding through miles of tents and across a half-dried swamp, we found a small camp in a field which had a board by the guard-tent marked "7a."

The sergeant of the guard pointed out to me the Camp Adjutant's tent and, leaving the draft in charge of Mulligan, I went across to it. The men were by this time wet to the skin and, as clean sheets and pyjamas were not included in their kit, or, as a matter of fact, any change of clothing except a pair of socks and a clean shirt, it looked as though they would most of them have pneumonia the next morning. However, one thing about active service is that it eliminates most of the minor worries of life. A man who may have a bullet through him before he is many days older is not very much afraid of catching cold when he is wet, and the men, when their tents were shown them, just shook the rain off their caps and turned inside.

The Camp Adjutant was a very fierce

individual, and when I inquired about a tent for Mulligan and myself said he did not think there was one; when I asked him what then it would be best for us to do, he was first blasphemous and then completely indifferent. A tent standing by itself behind the men's lines, he said, was a cavalry officer's tent, in fact, the whole camp was really a cavalry camp, and he did not know why the ―――― we had been sent there.

After he had gone I decided to go and look at the cavalry officer's tent. Pulling aside the flaps cautiously I peered inside and there saw, sitting on his valise and eating a biscuit with jam, a very immaculate young gentleman, with light, white-balled breeches and a large silver eagle on his cap. His head was bent as I looked in, but as he looked up I saw the pink and white, ingenious face of Herbert Beldhurst.

" Hullo ! " I said.

" Hullo ! " said Herbert, looking at me in polite perplexity, then, remembering who I was : " Oh, hullo ! Come inside."

I entered.

" Have a cigarette ? "

TAKING OUT A DRAFT 19

He produced a huge new leather campaigning cigarette case. Everything in his tent was new and designed, regardless of cost, to make campaigning as comfortable as possible. He had a smart spare saddle with two bright leather revolver holsters, a sandwich-case, a box of Fortnum and Mason's groceries, a special Burberry, and a gorgeous canary-yellow woollen waistcoat.

Hearing of our difficulty he at once offered me a share of his tent, and I had my kit put inside. Mulligan I left to look after himself, with implicit confidence in his power to do so.

Half an hour later Mulligan had billeted himself on two young officers fresh from Sandhurst, combined their rations with ours, and constituted himself president of a joint mess.

For the next few days we remained at the base camp waiting for orders to go up to the Front. The time was passed in route marching, inspecting arms and equipment, and trying to instil some sense of discipline into the draft. This last duty took some performing, as the draft resented being cooped up in the square acre of camp ground, and showed a disposition individually to go off into the town and get drunk.

One evening, about 7.30, an order came for the drafts for the 5th Division to entrain, and Mulligan and I and our 180 followers marched to the station.

That journey up to the Front was for me a never-to-be-forgotten experience. It lasted for three days, the train creeping along at ten miles an hour. As on the boat, we were a mixed party, comprising drafts for some eight regiments, and totalling about 1500 men. The train was of immense length. The senior officer was an elderly ex-Militia subaltern, completely incompetent. He made no regulations, posted no guards at stations, gave none of the draft officers orders, and by the end of the third day was firing his revolver wildly out of the window. For this I do not blame him much, for the situation had by this time reached a climax. The different drafts remained fairly quiet in their carriages for the first night, but when the next morning broke fine and sunny and we stopped at a station in the middle of a French town, first one man

TAKING OUT A DRAFT

and then another climbed down from the stuffy, crowded carriages on to the platform. From the platform it was only a step into the main street of the town, and this step was quickly taken. When the train wanted to move on there were no drafts. The drafts were all in cafés, cottages, and pie shops, receiving a hearty welcome from the inhabitants. The elderly ex-Militia subaltern said they must be collected and put back in the train, and set off with different draft officers to do this, but as fast as the men were turned out of one shop they went into another lower down the street. Eventually Mulligan organized a drive from the lower end of the town up to the station, the men were collected, and off we started again.

Warned by this experience, the ex-Militia subaltern ordered the driver of the train on no account again to stop near a town. Our next halt was, therefore, well in the middle of open country. Beside the line there ran a peaceful stream. The noonday heat was by now at its height, and after a glance out of the carriage windows we settled to sleep, secure in our remoteness from trouble.

Suddenly the ex-Militiaman, putting his head out of the window, exclaimed :

" My God ! Look at the ——s."

We looked, and saw several of the draft divesting themselves of their clothes preparing to bathe. We jumped out to order them into the train again, but while we were doing this every carriage was opened and the different drafts, perhaps thinking a bathing parade had been ordered and the officers were going down to superintend, all jumped out and made for the river.

" I should start the train again," said Mulligan, looking coldly on the scene of confusion. " They'll come back quick enough if they think they are going to be left behind."

The order was given, and with a long, warning whistle the train started slowly off. The effect was electrical. The men began to pour back at once. The train was kept going at two miles an hour, and those dressed were quickly on board again. One man, stark naked except for a pair of trousers, was left racing after her down the line holding up his trousers with one hand. He soon took a heavy toss over a switch wire, and the train

TAKING OUT A DRAFT 23

had to be stopped and a party sent back to fetch him. While this was happening the ex-Militia subaltern in charge, who was keeping an eagle look-out all along the train, spied another man making off. He called to him to stop, but the man apparently did not hear and continued. The distracted subaltern then called on a corporal in the next carriage to fire at the culprit with his rifle, which he did.

The victim, suddenly alive to his position, gave a wild yell when the shot was fired, and ran away as hard as he could. He disappeared into a wood and was never seen again.

Nearing Paris we began to pass hospital trains going west, and outside the city were halted alongside a train-load of German prisoners. They were a miserable, abject-looking lot, huddled together on the floors of the carriages, all in their muddy grey uniforms as they had been captured. I do not think in those days there was much hate in the heart of the British Tommy towards his foe, for our fellows threw them biscuits which they devoured ravenously, and cigarettes which they lit and passed round one to another with trembling hands.

The suburban trains were running into Paris with women, and men unfit for service or over military age, much as though business was going on as usual, but we were hardly beyond the outskirts before we were passing through ground which we were told the Germans had held a few weeks before, and the impression gathered was very different from any which could be derived within fifteen miles of London.

Beyond Paris we passed through some beautiful, thickly wooded country, and were told we were within thirty kilometres of the enemy. At one point we halted by a field-ambulance station. Here the wounded were brought down from behind the firing-line in motor ambulances, their wounds dressed, and then put on to a train. It was a stern first sight of war, that long barn strewn with straw and packed with groaning, blood-stained, muddy men straight from the trenches.

II. RAILHEAD AND BEYOND

FOR the last stage of the journey the train crawled very slowly. Very faintly in the distance we could hear the boom of guns. We looked at one another, Mulligan and I and the two lads from Sandhurst.

"We're getting into it now," said one of the Sandhurst boys.

"Yes—maybe this time twenty-four hours we shall be dead," said Mulligan with a grin.

In those days it did indeed happen that an officer only survived one day after reaching railhead. Some had been killed literally on their way to the trenches. However, Mulligan's cheery attitude of fatalism, combined with the sound of the guns, did not infect me with any wild good spirits, and I pulled out my pipe and filled it for the fifth time since lunch.

The four of us had been living for three days in the first-class carriage ever since we had entrained with our respective drafts at the base. We had slept, eaten, smoked, and made ourselves as comfortable as space would permit, and had also become very good friends. They were splendid boys, the two cadets from Sandhurst—one eighteen, the other nineteen. Theirs had been a short interval between the schoolboy and the man. A month after leaving the Royal Military College they had found themselves responsible officers sent out with a draft to their regiment in France. It had been instructive to watch the perfect self-possession of the boys and the way they handled their men. Now as we neared our journey's end they sat calmly looking out of the window, their ears pricked to catch the sound of the distant guns, liking the thought of war perhaps no more than others do when they find themselves very near to it, but perfectly self-possessed and prepared to do whatever was required of them. They have both given their lives for their country now, poor lads—such bits of life as they had to give, having passed through only two stages of it, and never known "the lover" or the full strength of man.

RAILHEAD AND BEYOND 27

At railhead the train stopped about half a mile outside the station. The railway transport officer came down the line to give us our instructions. He said he proposed to leave us in a siding for the night and we could have the train to ourselves, which would be better than turning out in a field to sleep. The men could light fires by the railway line for cooking, but they must not drink the water from a stream which ran alongside the line as it was unsafe. There were two wells from which water could be drawn for the troops a little way beyond a level-crossing further up the line. If each draft would send water-carrying parties they should be directed to the wells. He wished a guard put at the level-crossing to prevent any man walking up the line into the town. He was with us about four minutes giving his orders concisely, and so that they could be clearly understood; then he went back towards the station to attend to the multitude of duties which fall to the lot of a railway transport officer. He spoke without flurry or excitement and gave the impression, which every staff-officer should give, of being a thoroughly capable man who knew exactly what he wanted the troops he was handling to do.

When the R.T.O. had gone we went along the line to carry out the orders we had received. Having been explicitly told that the stream was poisoned and not fit to drink, and that all fires must be lit on the right side of the line and not on the left, some of the men proceeded to light fires on the wrong side of the railway and to fill their bottles from the stream. Having put these matters right by standing about and yelling at the offenders, and things having been put more or less in shape for the night, Mulligan and I went off into the town.

The town which lay deep down in a valley was in pitch darkness. There was no sign of life in the streets, except in the market square where some wagons were parked and a group of soldiers were sitting round the embers of a fire. Now and again large, silent motor-cars with officers wrapped up to the chin in overcoats and mufflers glided through. One of the men by the wagons told us that Sir John French had been in the town half an hour ago, had a quick consultation with some general officers, and passed on. In spite of the darkness, quiet, and

RAILHEAD AND BEYOND

absence of signs of activity, one felt somehow, as one stood in that market square with the shadowy wagons and group of men round the fire, that one had crossed the border and come into the zone of war. Railways were done with now and the infantry must take to their feet.

In view of certain reports we had heard about officers being picked off by specially detailed snipers, Mulligan and I had decided that at the first opportunity we would get rid of our brown leather belts and put on the web equipment worn by the men. Accordingly, when we got to the market square, we asked if there was any ordnance store in the town. A soldier directed us to a house at the corner of the square. We knocked on the door, and after a little difficulty roused the storeman, who took us into a large room where a quantity of clothing, equipment, and rifles collected from the dead, were piled on the floor. The storeman was a Royal Field Artilleryman, and he told us he was one of three survivors of a battery which had been left to fight a desperate rearguard action in the retreat from Mons—it was the battery in which all but one gun were put out of action. The man had a subdued manner and was reluctant to speak much of the engagement. To us, who had not yet seen a shell burst, this meeting with a man who had been through so much fighting was significant. We took our web equipment and made our way back to the train.

The morning broke fine and sunny, and we turned out along the line quite ready to march. As we were putting on the web equipment we had collected over night, the French driver of the train came along. He stopped and looked at us curiously, then asked why we were discarding our officer's belts and putting on men's equipment. We explained it was because we did not want to be picked out as officers. He said: " With our officers it is the same uniform in peace as in war." I could not think of an adequate reply to this, but the natural and irritable one would have been " more fools they," which Mulligan made without any hesitation. However, the engine driver's remark rankled, and as the R.T.O. said that most of the officers he had seen had gone up to the front in their Sam Browne belts, we decided to do the same after all and pack the web equipment in our kit.

RAILHEAD AND BEYOND 31

We got our orders to march at noon. Mulligan and I with our draft and the draft for another regiment were to start first; the two Sandhurst lads, who were going to another brigade, were to wait till the afternoon. We sorted out our different drafts, wished them good-bye, and set off.

Part of the way from railhead to divisional headquarters lay over a ridge which overlooked the valley of the Aisne. From this ridge we saw our first shells bursting at a comfortable distance of some two mile away. One wondered as one watched the little white puffs of smoke which appeared suddenly and noiselessly, hovered for a minute a score of feet above the earth, and blew away, what damage they had caused and what it must be like for the men who formed the target beneath them.

The valley of the Aisne, as we saw it, except for those white puffs of smoke and the occasional distant boom of a heavy gun, showed no signs of war. The fields were quiet and empty as on a Sunday, with crops growing tranquilly and here and there a stack of hay. At one point we passed an artillery supply park with an imperturbable-looking gunner subaltern, with an eyeglass, and a major in charge. The major had a large scale-map of the area, and showed me from it where our lines and the German's lines lay, pointing out the actual places on the horizon.

He was passing the time making out possible phases of battles to come from the map. The subaltern told us that the word "Uhlan" (in the early days of the war often heard) was extinct as a form of terrorism, for, he said, they and their horses were half-starved, and turned and bolted on sight.

After some five miles march we arrived at divisional headquarters, which consisted of the principal house in a tiny village. Here I found an officer in my regiment who was attached to the staff, and who asked me to come in and have tea while he found out what I was to do with the men I had brought out from England.

The general and his staff were having tea round a deal table in the front room of the house when I went in and all greeted me kindly. Tea consisted of bread, jam, and tea without milk. There was no butter, only two or three plates, and some brown sugar in

RAILHEAD AND BEYOND 33

a paper bag. The meal belied any impression I may have had of the luxury in which generals and their staff were wont to live in war time.

There was a discussion among the staff officers as to what they were to do with the draft and myself and Mulligan. One was for sending us down to the trenches that night, another for keeping us back in reserve. I personally hoped for a night in peace and quiet, and I could see that the staff officer who was in favour of keeping us in reserve thought it would be rather a severe experience for a draft to be sent down into the trenches the first night they arrived at the front.

Eventually it was decided that we should go to our second line transport which lay some two miles behind the firing-line, and with directions as to the road we started off. It was by this time dark; however, we had no difficulties until we came to the village where our second line transport was supposed to be. This village was packed with troops, and from no one could we get information about the whereabouts of our second line transport. There followed an hour of hopeless wandering and questioning, while Mulligan and I cursed the army and everything to do with the army (with especial reference to the staff) for fools and worse. At one point we came into collision with a regiment marching out to take its turn in the trenches. The officers all were wearing Burberrys and mufflers, and had greatcoats rolled on their backs. The men were carrying little pots for cooking, extra bandoliers of ammunition, and other things likely to be useful to them in the trenches. All looked prepared to be thoroughly uncomfortable.

At last, after some further wandering, we struck boldly out on a road along which we were told we should find our second line transport. I was a little uneasy as we left the village behind us and marched out into the darkness, for I knew we were going in the direction of the enemy, and it would be a never-to-be-forgotten episode in an officer's career to lead a draft of reinforcements fresh from England straight into the hands of the enemy instead of to their regiment. However, before we had gone far a voice greeted me cheerily and I discovered our quartermaster.

"You come with me, I'll take you to the transport. Now then, lads, close up there,"

RAILHEAD AND BEYOND 35

he said, in the crisp, businesslike voice I had often heard on the parade-ground in times of peace when he was regimental sergeant-major.

Only those young officers who served in the days before the war, and learnt to lean a little on the " backbone " of the army, can understand the relief it was to me, after a fortnight's responsibility with the 180 rascals who formed my draft, to feel them gripped once again by the voice of an old regular ex-non-commissioned officer.

Under Clay's guidance the draft followed like sheep into the courtyard of a farm, and stood quietly in their ranks while we went into the building. In the centre of the yard a fire was burning and the sergeant-cook was busy preparing supper (this would have been too much for the draft altogether if they had been alone with me). The sergeant-cook shook my hand warmly in his huge red paw and wished me luck on joining the regiment on active service. He then busied himself preparing a dixie of tea for the men. Inside the farm I found Sergeant Mace, the officers' mess sergeant, in khaki and shirt sleeves but just as anxious that the officers should have everything they wanted as he had been when his portly chest had been covered by a glossy white shirt. He brought me a cup of tea, unearthed from the mess van a bottle of rum, poured it liberally into the tea, and went out with some bread, dripping, and eggs to fry some supper over the fire in the yard.

Of the welcomes I have had I shall always remember the first night when I reached the second line transport of my regiment in France.

Thinking to remain with the transport that night, Mulligan and I had found some straw for the draft and were sitting on biscuit boxes over the fire drinking hot rum and water, and hearing the gossip of the regiment from Clay and Mace before turning in, when an orderly arrived with orders. We were to go down into the trenches that night.

Clay said it was rough luck we should not get one night's rest. He was also extremely matter of fact. He roused the men from their slumbers in a trice, cursed a man roundly who dropped his rifle, harangued the draft in a hoarse whisper, telling them that they were going to be sent

RAILHEAD AND BEYOND 37

across to the other side of the river into the firing-line, and that if they made a noise they would get a German battery turned on them, said a few words to Mulligan and myself aside, advising one of us to keep at the head of the company and one behind, and to keep the men well closed up, as if fire was suddenly opened at night on troops just out of England it might be touch and go what would happen, and said good-bye to us, without—as I thought, considering the occasion—much tenderness.

It was pitch dark when we started off from the transport to go down to the firing-line. The transport sergeant came with us to show the way and marched with me at the head of the draft. He told me that he had to take the supply-wagon down every night to the regiment, and that it was a job he was glad to have over for the day. That morning he had been late returning, and day was breaking as he crossed the river. Three shells had been fired, two narrowly missing his wagon. I could see he was rather shaken by his morning's experience and that he did not particularly relish the task of piloting down the draft. However, never having seen any shells burst, they had no terror for me, and I rather enjoyed the quiet sense of adventure which hung over the expedition.

After half a mile we left the main road and crossed the pontoon bridge. From this point onwards our way lay across the fields. In the darkness we could see nothing and had no compass to give the direction. The transport sergeant picked his way by keeping to a muddy track which had been worn across the fields and stubble by troops passing to and fro from the firing-line to the rear. Whenever our boots stopped squelching and slipping back we knew we were off the track and groped about till we were back in the mud and cart-ruts again.

A few months afterwards when I read that the French troops, who had taken over our line when the British Army was moved up to Flanders, had had to retire to the high ground south of the Aisne owing to the impossibility of keeping up communication with their line across the river when the winter rain came, I remembered that muddy, slippery walk and understood their difficulties.

We had been going for what seemed quite an hour when we came to a large hay shed. Here we halted as the sergeant said he was not quite sure where we were wanted, but that the trenches were quite near. It was late, the men tired, and the hay-shed presented at any rate a certainty of shelter and some warmth, so I decided to remain there for the night.

III. EARLY DAYS ON THE AISNE

THERE was a big difference between the first and second occasions on which I joined my regiment.

The first time was as a Sandhurst cadet and I joined a regiment at full strength of officers and men. I remember we sat down to dinner that night some twenty of us, and being bewildered by all the faces and trying to make out which was the colonel and wondering if I should ever learn the names of all the different subalterns and captains. The mess table was laden with silver and outside a band in scarlet tunics played.

The second time was when I rejoined after a year's absence on the outbreak of war, and went with Mulligan and the draft to join them in the trenches on the Aisne. By then they had fought at Mons, Le Cateau, and the Marne.

The Adjutant, who met me behind the lines to take me to the Commanding Officer, prepared me a little for what to expect.

EARLY DAYS ON THE AISNE 41

"Blain is commanding," he said, as we threaded our way single file down a path through a wood. Blain, I knew, had been a very junior captain a month before when war broke out.

The Adjutant proceeded to explain:

"The Colonel and Ames were hit at Mons." (Ames was the senior major.) Johnson and Hewett (another major and a captain) had been hit on the Marne. "Clark and Sergeant Johnson—you remember Johnson?" I nodded, well remembering Clark's inimitable colour-sergeant—the pair had been inseparable and the officer greatly dependent on the man for the keeping of his company accounts, etc., in the days of peace—"were killed the day before yesterday. They are buried together by that farm." The Adjutant softened his voice from the tone of matter-of-fact recital as he pointed to a farm building through the trees.

"Well, here we are," he said as we came to a little straw and earth shelter in the wood. "Here's some fresh blood, sir," he said, to a youthful looking captain sitting on a tree stump outside the shelter. This was Blain, who through the accidents of war was now left in command of the regiment. There were left, besides, one other captain and some half-dozen subalterns. Of these the scout officer and machine-gun officer were with Blain, the others out in command of their companies in the trenches.

"Hullo!" said Blain, holding out his hand. "We are going to put you with Goyle's company."

I grinned as unconcernedly as I could. So Goyle was one of the survivors, then. Goyle was the regimental fire-eater. He had been longing for this war for years and was more pleased than many others I knew when it actually happened. To be Goyle's subaltern on active service, I had always surmised, was to have guarantee of plenty of fighting.

If ever a reluctant youth found himself holding out against overwhelming odds in an impossible position it would be one of Goyle's subalterns.

"Goyle has had bad luck with his subalterns," said Blain. "He has lost four."

"I hope he doesn't lose me," I said with some sincerity.

Blain and the Adjutant laughed. "Well,

EARLY DAYS ON THE AISNE 43

we'll send you on up to him," said the former. "Let's see—I think he has got the forward trench to-day."

"Yes, he has," said the Adjutant; then, turning to me, "You'll be near enough to them for your first day in the trenches—two hundred yards."

I grinned again as genially as possible.

"Have some breakfast before you go up," said the C.O., handing me a biscuit and a pot of jam and pointing to a pannikin of tea.

It was very damp in the wood. The trees were dripping. The tea was cold. The party, with Blain as C.O., and the Adjutant and two subalterns, were a forlorn little group to be left out of a regiment. All had rather a strained air, and my good spirits and feeling of being fresh out from England were evidently not infectious to men who had been through what they had. They had had a shell near them already that morning and were all frankly apprehensive of another. From that moment any ideas I may have had about the pleasures and excitements of active service left me, and I merely wondered what sort of a trench I was going to and what Fate might have to bring me on my first day of active service.

I had always imagined that trenches were only approached by night, and then by crawling on one's belly along narrow communication passages. But we set off in broad daylight, at eight in the morning, to go up to our trench. The reason we were able to do this was because the trenches on the Aisne were along the edges of woods, and it was possible to move through the trees right up to within two hundred yards of the enemy without being observed.

The advanced trench which Goyle was holding with his company lay in a small wood, rather in advance of the main line of trenches. The path which led to it twisted and twined and branched off into other paths so confusedly that I wondered how the Adjutant could find his way. The actual trench itself consisted in a bank along the edge of the wood in which a chain of dug-outs had been excavated. We found Goyle in a dug-out in the centre, which was distinguished from the others by some straw and a couple of waterproof sheets; there was also a wooden box

EARLY DAYS ON THE AISNE 45

without a lid, in which the officers' rations were kept. Goyle was sitting in the dug-out with Evans, his remaining subaltern, and having taken me thus far, the Adjutant returned to the C.O.

Evans was an old friend of mine and fellow-subaltern. We talked together for a while and then he showed me cautiously how to creep up to the top of the parapet and look through some long grass at the enemy's trenches 200 yards away, and he told me the story of the fight for the position we now held and where so-and-so, and so-and-so—brother officers whom I'd seen leave England a month before with a cheery wave of the hand for me and a joke about meeting " out there " soon— had been killed the day before.

At nine o'clock we rummaged in our ration-box and made breakfast off jam and biscuits and cheese. It was quite pleasant in the dug-out and there was no sound of war. As we were making our breakfast a shot rang out and there was a piercing yell.

"Hullo! they must have got one of the fellows I put on sentry at the edge of the wood," said Goyle, helping himself to more jam.

"Is that one of our fellows?" he called to the sergeant.

"Yessir—hit in the buttocks, sir"; the sergeant slapped the portly part of himself on which he sat.

We all laughed.

The yell gave way to groans—loud, long, and terrible.

I looked as unconcerned as possible and dipped my own biscuit into the pot. "Tell that fellow to stop making such a noise," said Captain Jones, angrily putting his head round the dug-out.

I felt myself that it was a pity the Germans should know the good result of their shooting and that the fellow ought not to make such a fuss. However, the groaning went on as loudly as ever, and at last Jones got up exasperated to go and see what was the matter.

He came back with a grave face.

"Only hit in his 'sit-upon,' wasn't he?" My fellow-subaltern looked up smiling.

"H'm, it's worse—went through and has lodged somewhere in his intestines," and murmuring "in agony, poor fellow!" Cap-

EARLY DAYS ON THE AISNE 47

tain Jones looked to see if we had emptied the jam-pot while he was away.

It did not take more than an hour or two to pick up the rudiments of trench life. We passed the morning sitting in the dug-out, reading a few old papers and smoking and talking. By eleven the sun was high enough to peep in over the top of the parapet and warm us, and it all seemed to me a very pleasant, lazy sort of existence. There was no firing except for an occasional " ping " from a sniper Goyle kept posted at the corner of the trench, and an answering shot or two from the German side. Rifle fire seemed a matter of tacit arrangement. When our sniper was joined by a friend, or fired two or three times in a minute instead of once every three or four, the German fire grew brisker and life in the trench less tranquil. Our sniper was thereupon reproved by Goyle and was silent, whereupon the German fire died down.

At midday Goyle suggested we should lunch, and Evans pulled the wooden box towards him. He gave us out each two large square army biscuits and opened a small tin of bully beef, which he turned out on a piece of paper and cut into three portions. The beef and biscuits did not make a bad meal at all, but the best was to follow. Goyle produced from his haversack a tin cup, and from the box a wine-bottle about a third full. He then mixed a tot of rum with the same quantity of water in the cup and drank, passing on the emptied cup to Evans, who took his share; after I had had mine there was just enough left for us each to have half a cup more. How delicious that rum was! I rolled myself a cigarette, lay back in the straw, and basked contentedly. I felt comfortable and warm and drowsy.

Away in the distance one could hear the booming of big guns which went on all day, but this was the only thing to remind one that one was in the middle of the battle of the Aisne. I saw Evans opposite me lean back and close his eyes, and remember thinking Goyle was rather energetic to sit so bolt upright all the time.

It was a sound of firing that woke me. Phizz — Phizz — Phizz! through the leaves above and some sharp cracks from our men. Goyle and Evans were still sitting where they

EARLY DAYS ON THE AISNE

had lunched, listening intently. I sat up, too, wondering what was going on. " Were we being attacked or what was happening ? " I asked Goyle, who replied briefly that he did not know.

" Just take No. 8 platoon and line that trench along the end there," he said to Evans. Evans got up and crept out of the dug-out along towards the sound of firing.

" Very exposed here," muttered Goyle to himself. " C.O. said if this point went the whole line would go too."

" Um ! " I thought to myself, now quite alive to being in the middle of a battle.

" Are you all right ? " a voice called. We looked out and saw the C.O. standing in the wood behind us. He had come running up as soon as he heard the firing. I have always remembered him running up like that to see if all was well. Many commanding officers would have thought it best to remain at their headquarters and let reports come in to them from the different companies.

It gave one great confidence to see him standing there calmly. Then suddenly the firing died down.

"Don't think it was anything," said Goyle, "but it is rather a nasty place this; we could not do much if they tried to rush us. I'll keep that platoon out along the flank there for a bit."

"You're going to be relieved to-night," said the C.O. "The Gloucesters are taking over from us."

At ten o'clock that night the company of the regiment which was relieving us filed slowly into our trenches. As each of the new platoons got into position the old platoon made its way out to the place where it had been directed to halt. There could be no talking or asking of questions as the enemy were two hundred yards away, but the simple and explicit instructions which Goyle had given to the platoon commanders in the afternoon enabled the whole movement to be carried out correctly. The section-commander of the leading section of each platoon had to keep in touch with the section commander of the rear section of the platoon in front of him, and by this plan of following my leader the whole company moved as one man in the darkness along the intricate paths which intersected the wood.

By eleven o'clock we had arrived safely at our destination—a clearing in the wood about half a mile behind the front trenches. There we found a series of little straw houses made by the last regiment, wide enough to hold six men laying down and high enough to allow a man to sit up in them. We selected one of these bivouacs for ourselves and distributed the men among the remainder. I so far had escaped having to spend a night in the trenches, but to the men, who had been where I joined them that morning for three days and nights, the bivouacs were a great comfort. The mere relief of tension, which the extra six hundred yards or so we had put between ourselves and the enemy afforded, was appreciated by all, and being now well screened from view we could move about as we liked. Evans told me that Goyle had hardly slept at all any of the three nights, but spent the whole time going round seeing that the sentries were alert and at their posts. After we had chosen our bivouac and put down our haversacks and water-bottles to mark the place where we proposed to sleep, the question arose of supper. We had very little of our day's rations left—however, I saw a dim light peeping from a bivouac which stood by itself, and guessing it meant a party, went across to investigate. Here I found the other officers of the regiment lying round on straw discussing a cold leg of mutton and some bread which had been sent down from the transport. I claimed and was given a share for Goyle, Evans, and myself, and also a small extra tot of rum. Nothing tastes nicer than cold meat and bread when one is hungry, and with the rum and mutton inside us and a few whiffs of a pipe we were soon fast asleep.

We slept till well after six the next morning, and when we woke the sun was breaking through the mist which always haunts the valley of the Aisne at dawn. By nine a glorious autumn day had fully broken. We had two canteens of steaming tea and cold bacon for breakfast. Goyle then produced some cleaning traps and began a prodigious toilet. He shaved himself, he washed his teeth, he soaped his head and plunged it into a bucket of cold water; finally he took off his trousers and poured the water over himself. Then he had a rub down with a tiny towel, put on his trousers and shirt again, and sat down under a tree, saying he felt better. Evans and I, unshaven, muddy, but feeling quite warm and comfortable, watched all this rather cynically.

"Always wash when you get the chance," said Goyle, who, having been through the South African War, played the rôle of old campaigner.

It seemed to me that it would be time enough to wash the next day when we were to go back to billets. However, after half an hour Evans sent for a bucket of water, washed himself, and declared he felt much fresher. He then joined Goyle under the tree and combed his hair. I began to feel a dirty fellow, and finally borrowing Goyle's soap and towel, washed too.

We passed the day very happily sitting about and sleeping in the sun. At dusk we got orders to move and go and improve some entrenchments.

As soon as it was dark the regiment paraded and moved off, with orders to dig till midnight and then rest and cross the Aisne an hour before dawn.

The place assigned to my company for digging was a ditch running along a fence facing the hills on the enemy's side of the river. The enemy had their trenches on the slopes of these hills, and it seemed funny to be digging under their noses, as it were, under cover of darkness. Evidently the night was good enough cover, for not a shot was fired to disturb us at our work. I noticed, however, that Goyle ran no risks, but made each man lay his equipment and rifle exactly in front of him so that the different working parties could be transformed into a firing-line at an instant's notice. The men worked away with a will as unconcerned as if they were digging a potato patch. The only thing which worried them a little was a searchlight which the enemy continually flashed across the front of their lines. At first the men could not get used to this light, but threw themselves flat on the ground whenever it appeared in their direction, but as the enemy never fired, apparently the searchlight revealed nothing to them. Evans and I studied this light for a

EARLY DAYS ON THE AISNE 55

little while and then discovered that a knoll lay between it and us, and hid us from its direct rays so that we were all perfectly safe. As a matter of fact Goyle explained that if a man did come into the direct ray of a searchlight, he would only look like the stump of a tree or a shrub to the observer if he stood still. It was by movement alone that he betrayed himself. However, it requires a certain amount of confidence to stand quite still when caught by a searchlight and not try to move away or hide behind a tree. This confidence the men who were not hidden by the knoll lacked at first ; in fact, they had a great dislike for the searchlight and were inclined to be reproachful because we had no searchlights ourselves. Thomas Atkins is a keen critic of the art of war, and such things as well-placed searchlights and the superior number of the enemy's machine-guns do not escape his notice. He likes to feel that he has been given as good a start as the man he is fighting against, and it would have been interesting to have heard the comments of our men in the trenches when the Germans first started to employ gas.

At midnight we knocked off digging and

retired to a field to sleep. It is extremely cold in the Aisne valley on autumn nights, and the dew-drenched ground did not look inviting. The men were told to lie down where they were, and as it began to dawn on them that no further arrangements were to be made for their comfort, they grinned rather expressively in a way they have when they wish to be quite pleasant but at the same time feel they have a lot to put up with.

I happened to have noticed the field as we passed it on our way to entrench, and to remember that at the top there were several sheaves of corn. Accordingly, when all was quiet, I sent the men of my platoon up two at a time to fetch some of these sheaves down and also to bring me three for myself. Spreading out one underneath me and the other two over my feet and chest I soon was as warm as if I'd been between blankets. It was a glorious night, and it was grand to be there in the warm straw looking up at the stars. About four I was awoken by a sound of stamping, and looking sideways saw the men who had no straw stamping to keep themselves warm and looking reproachfully at my platoon who were all lying snug and comfortable like a litter of puppies. Soon after this the order came to move and we crossed back over the Aisne as day was breaking. The slow-running, mist-hung river was a peaceful-looking object to give a name to a battlefield, but the putting up of the pontoon bridge by which we crossed had cost many men their lives and brought to one the V.C.

IV. IN BILLETS

THE village where we were to billet lay a mile on the other side of the river in a deep quiet valley. The Quartermaster and transport officer met us half a mile from our destination. They were both unaffectedly glad to see the regiment coming back into safety for a while, though, alas, there were only two-thirds of the officers left who had crossed the river a week before. It was a trying time for the Quartermaster and transport subaltern, when the regiment went into action. They had to stay behind, with only occasional fleeting visits to the firing-line, often for as long as a week or ten days. When there was a big attack, and the air for miles on either side was filled with one reverberating crash of gun and rifle fire, they had to bear the strain which is always more acute for those within sound but not in sight of fighting.

"I've got a fine breakfast for you," said the Quartermaster, "bacon and eggs and sausages."

We were glad to hear it. Meals for the

IN BILLETS

past week had been scrappy affairs. Since we had parted company with our transport we had none of us tasted a hot dish of any description. Cold bacon and bread for breakfast, cold bully and cheese for lunch, cold bully and cheese again for supper. Good enough nourishment, of course, for anyone, and nice enough at the time to eat, but still a real steaming dish of bacon and eggs did sound delicious.

We soon came to the village where the brigade was to be billeted in reserve. It lay in a curve of a winding valley which ran down into the main valley of the river. The billets were allotted by companies, so much cottage and farm space being given to each company commander for his company. To those who read these lines in England the quarters allotted to men back for a few days rest from trenches may not sound very grand. My company had, for instance, a stable, two farm outbuildings, and a sort of underground cellar which was approached by a narrow arch—to crawl through which the men had to go on hands and knees—and which looked just like the kennels of a pack of foxhounds. The stable, the cellar, and the outhouses were bare except for a layer of straw. However, to the men these places seemed amply satisfying. They meant warmth at night, shelter from rain, and soft dry lying. It was the first rest the men had had for some while. Many of them had lost their greatcoats, cardigans, and woollen underclothing, owing to the exigencies of actual fighting, and had had nothing to add to their scanty clothing as they lay out in the open during the cold nights. They crowded joyfully into their billets as Goyle and I and Evans went round allotting so much space to each platoon.

Having arranged for the men we now looked round for quarters for ourselves. Goyle, whose natural inclinations for Spartan simplicity were being rapidly fanned to a mania by active service, suggested that he and Evans and I should share the stone-slabbed floor of the lower room of a cottage which looked out on a manure yard. Evans, always anxious to please, was quite agreeable to this, and set to work with a broom to sweep out the yard, but I broke away from the arrangements and went to look for quarters for myself.

After a short search I came on Mulligan,

IN BILLETS 61

who had found some quite good quarters in a cottage. He had got a small bedroom leading off the owner's room, and suggested that the apple-loft on the same floor would do for me if I had one of the mattresses from his bed. I therefore sent Jenkins for my kit and set up house with him.

The 35-lb. kit which officers are allowed to keep with the transport meets all requirements on active service. As first bought and taken out from England it is a most immaculate and neatly arranged affair, but after a fortnight's jolting around in the wagons and a few hurried packings and unpackings it becomes a mere bundle containing a few cherished necessities. My valise held a sleeping-bag, two shirts, two pairs of socks, a pair of boots, a pair of trousers, some slippers, a few sticks of chocolate and a tin of tobacco. However, as Jenkins unpacked I watched it with the complacency of a man regarding his home. A bucket of cold water and a canteen of hot were next produced, and from the sleeping-bag my toilet set—razor, shaving brush, cake of soap, comb, and toothbrush—wrapped in a towel; and removing my coat and boots and puttees

I sat down on the valise and shaved. A bath followed in the bucket and then getting into clean socks and shirt and putting on the clippers and trousers for greater comfort, I combed my hair and surveyed myself with satisfaction in a small pocket mirror. Burnt by the sun and hardened by outdoor life, I certainly have never felt fitter in all my life.

It was now about noon, and Mulligan and I strolled across to the mess. The mess consisted chiefly of " Black Maria," a small lumbering van which the mess sergeant had bought for two pounds in Belgium at the beginning of the war, and which carried all our provisions. We were only able to gather round " Black Maria " at such times of comparative peace as being in billets or on the march behind the firing-line, but her presence on the scene always meant a scale of meals and comfort undreamed of in the trenches. Bacon and eggs came from her inside, and joints and vegetables, cocoa, tea, jam, bread, butter, biscuits, also vermouth, whisky and other stimulating drinks. It was wonderful the amount she held.

We found " Black Maria " had been drawn

IN BILLETS 63

up in the yard of a farm. A long trestle-table was set outside the front door of the farm, and several officers were sitting round this untying parcels and reading letters which had been sent out in a mail from England.

Over a fire on the far side of " Black Maria " the mess sergeant and his assistants were cooking lunch.

With the parcels which had just arrived from England there was now a plentiful supply of cigarettes, tobacco, socks, and underclothing for everybody, and while we sat waiting for lunch various exchanges were made between officers : a pair of socks for twenty-five cigarettes, an electric torch for a new briar pipe, and so on. Others, who had more of the same things sent than they wanted, put them into a box reserved for general use, from which any officer could take anything that he wanted. The parcels of officers who had been wounded and gone home were opened unceremoniously and their contents divided among the survivors.

With letters from wives and sweethearts and friends in their pockets, plenty of newspapers and parcels, and the thought of having nothing to do for the next day or two, everybody was in the best of tempers at luncheon. True, there were gaps now round the table, gaps which had not been there a few days ago, and which each was causing its measure of desolation to some English home, but by the men who had come through and learnt to bow their heads to the laws of chance and feel thankful that they too had not been taken, these gaps were not felt keenly—it was all a part of war, just as being in billets was. A day or two ago the men round the table had been in the woods across the river fighting : then the gaps had been made : that had been no joke—now they were sitting comfortably in the sun with food before them such as they had not seen for a fortnight. It would be silly not to eat and be merry.

My apple-loft proved a most comfortable chamber, and I lost no time after dinner in throwing off my clothes, getting into pyjamas, and rolling myself up in my sleeping-bag. In the middle of the night as it seemed—or to be precise, at 4 A.M.—I was woken by Jenkins. He bore the unwelcome news that the regiment was to be on the march in a quarter of an hour.

IN BILLETS 65

He added that he had heard a report that the Germans had broken through our line somewhere, and that the whole brigade was turning out. It was an affair of three minutes to get into my clothes and equipment, which I kept ready laid out beside me. While I was dressing, Jenkins deftly rolled and strapped my valise, and off he went with it to the transport wagon while I hurried to my company. The company had already turned out when I arrived, and the men were standing outside their billets. Five minutes later we had formed fours and were swinging out of the village. It was quick work at night to turn a whole brigade out of billets at twenty minutes notice, for to wake 4000 sleeping men, scattered all over a village, and get each in his proper place complete with arms and equipment in that space of time, is no easy task. In peace time the operation would have taken at least three hours, for the men would not have exactly lent themselves to the project, but in war all is vastly different. The alarm proved false, and after marching for a mile we were halted and finally marched home again, this time for five days of unbroken rest.

The days passed pleasantly enough. There were so many little luxuries which could be indulged in in billets. It was good to go about feeling washed, and delightful to wake up in the morning feeling one had had a good night's rest, drink a cup of tea in bed, and then roll a cigarette and smoke it as one shaved squatting on one's mattress. Breakfast would follow at the table outside the farm—breakfast of eggs and bacon and as much tea and bread and butter and jam as one wanted. Then a visit to the company and an inspection of the men's rifles or their kit, perhaps a journey to the Quartermaster to try and get a man another pair of boots or a coat which he wanted. The men nearly all needed one thing or another renewed, and from where we were we could get fresh supplies up from the base. It was a pleasure to see the joy a man took in a new cardigan waistcoat or a clean pair of socks and a shirt. He had probably worn his old ragged things uncomplainingly for three weeks, but now he strutted about round the billets patting his chest and showing off the new waistcoat or boots to his pals.

At midday a mail often came in with packets

IN BILLETS

of letters and parcels for everybody, and the letters had to be answered and the parcels opened and their contents shown round.

Then we did a little entertaining with the other regiments of the brigade, and staff officers would come down with bits of gossip and information about the general situation which we never got a chance of learning in the trenches. There was one fellow, an intelligence officer—heaven knows what has become of him now—who came to dine with us one night before going on to the trenches. His was most difficult and dangerous work, as he used to go out at nights, crawl out beyond our trenches and find out the position of the enemy's wire entanglements and advanced posts. It was the joke to tell him that a place would be laid for him at breakfast on his way back to general headquarters the next morning, and glad we all were when he came back to fill it.

Sometimes after tea we would go for short excursions to the country round. It was very beautiful country, and from the high ground on either side of the valley it was possible to get a far-reaching view of the battlefield.

68 WITH MY REGIMENT

Some evenings there seemed no sign of war, and one evening in particular I remember when I had gone out with Mulligan to explore a village on the hill above us. The village was built of grey stone hewn from a quarry in the hillside. Most of the inhabitants had stayed in their homes although the Germans had at one time been through their village. They told us how the Uhlans had ridden through in a great hurry, snatching what they wanted, but happily unable to stay to carry out coarse threats, and how the British cavalry had followed hot on their heels. But all this had been some while ago, and for the past weeks the village had been in peace. The church had some beautiful stained-glass windows which were all shivered by the explosion of shells, but the building itself stood intact, and Mulligan and I went inside and stepped softly up the aisle, unswept since war began, and littered with fragments of plaster from the ceiling. There was a great sense of calm and dignity about the little church, which had remained so near the battlefield a quiet place of refuge for its people. The old priest came across from his cottage and, bowing to us

IN BILLETS 69

ceremoniously, offered us each a pear. We walked with him through the village till we came to a point beyond, from which we could see right down into the valley where the two armies lay facing each other. The sun was just setting at the further end of the valley and the evening mists were curling low over the meadows and river. Somewhere away behind a bell tolled for a service. For a few minutes as we stood there all was peace and quiet, then from the hill opposite our guns opened fire. The shells went screaming across the valley tearing their way through the soft evening air. We watched, wondering what was their target. Then suddenly flames broke out from a village lying across the valley within the enemy's lines. Looking through our glasses we could see the flames came from some stacks near a farm. *Crash—Crash—Crash!* Shell after shell fell among the cottages. Slowly the flames spread as one building after another was set aflame. The sun had sunk now and the sky was darkening. The whole village seemed one crackling bonfire. Still our guns hurled shells into the flames. Their fire seemed merciless as they lashed the little village with round after round. Suddenly the firing stopped. It had grown dark. The village was blazing now fiercely, and the whole sky was red. The work of the guns was done. We stood a moment watching the lurid, glowing mass. Mulligan wondered if we had caught a nest full of German troops. The old priest said nothing : it was war. Gradually the flames grew less, and only here and there bright red patches reflected themselves against heavy clouds of smoke. Saying good-night to the priest we made our way slowly back to billets.

V. THE MOVE UP (1)

WE had been in our billets in the village behind the Aisne a week when the order came to move. It came suddenly one evening at seven o'clock, as orders do at the Front, and by seven-thirty we were on the march. Where to, why, or for how long no one had any idea. Perhaps we were moving to a threatened point of the line, perhaps troops were being concentrated for an attack, perhaps the whole division, which had suffered heavily since the outbreak of war, was being replaced by a fresh division and was being sent back to the base to refit, reorganize, and fill its gaps.

As we marched along we attempted to make deductions from the direction we were taking. One thing was plain, the road led directly back from the line of the river and the enemy. It might be, of course, that after going a mile or two we should swing right-handed and move along parallel to the enemy but out of reach of their guns till we came behind some point where we were wanted, and then be moved up again. We climbed up out of the valley and crossed a high plateau of waste land. Goyle told me that the German rearguard of horse artillery and cavalry had dashed pell-mell across this plateau in their retreat from the Marne, hotly pursued by our cavalry and guns, pausing at intervals to exchange shots with their pursuers, crashing on down the valley and across the Aisne, where they had made the stand they had maintained ever since. It must have been a fine sight to have seen the pursuer and pursued crossing the plateau.

Four or five miles back we passed some troops bivouacking by a farm.

" What are you ? " called Goyle.

" The ——s," came a rather sullen answer.

It was the —— Regiment—all that was left of it—perhaps a hundred men. They had been badly cut up a few days before, and, no longer existing as a regiment, had been withdrawn from the firing-line.

A mile or two further on we came to the end of our journey for that day—a village where we were to billet. Our billeting officer had gone ahead, and we had not long to wait

THE MOVE UP

in the road before he came to show the company their billeting area. In the darkness it took a little time to get the men settled. They naturally resented being put in pigsties, which Edwards, who had no sense of smell and only felt the straw with his feet, tried to do with his platoon. Then Mulligan, who was always a bit hot on these occasions, annexed a barn, which was just within our boundary, for A Company, and, successful in this, attempted to take over a kitchen right in the heart of our area for the use of A Company officers.

When I went to eject him from this he adopted the tone, " We must all share in on service," and as I still preserved a stony countenance, obtruded the nose of a bottle of rum from his haversack and said we would have some hot toddy when all was quiet, whereupon, on striking a bargain that I should have the bed and he a mattress from it on the floor, I let him remain.

Some electric torches we had had sent out from England were of the greatest use at times like this, as they enabled us to flash them into the interior of barns and get the men properly settled in places where there was room for them and where they could sleep in comfort. Also, as we were well away from the firing-line, we could have " Black Maria," our mess van, with us, and hot meals when we got in and before we started in the morning.

We remained in the village all the next day, moving off just before nightfall the following evening. During the day I went to pay a visit to some of the other units of the brigade. The Westshires were billeted further down the village, and had passed the night as comfortably as ourselves, but the Dorchesters had not been so fortunate, and had had to sleep in a field, as there had been no billeting space left for them. Greatly conscious of the warm bed I had just left, I surveyed with a sympathy which they did not seem to appreciate the little "boovey-hutches" and lairs of straw which they had made for themselves. The artillery, too, had had to sleep out, to be near their guns and horses, and were in a bad temper. One young artillery officer was very sarcastic about the mystery which was being made of our movements—the marching by night and hiding

THE MOVE UP 75

by day with no hint as to destination—and said several unflattering things about red tape, brass hat rims, and other insignia of staff. He was an amusing fellow with his wit sharpened to the point of acidity by the cold cheerless night he had spent in the open, and I stood listening to him for some time. I could imagine him standing between his section of guns directing their fire in the early days of the retreat, when the enemy pressed on us in their masses and every gun had to fire while there was a man left to work it. He would probably have been very witty and deliberate about the objective of the last shell.

Our second night march was longer than the first, and we covered eighteen miles. We appeared still to be going farther and farther away from the enemy, but at one point, nearing the end of the march, we heard faintly the sound of guns. They were the French guns, we were told, so we gathered that we were somewhere behind the French lines. A long climb down took us to a bridge over a river, guarded by a very bored-looking French reservist who looked at us suspiciously, and was, I felt sure, longing for the excuse for a row with somebody, just to relieve the monotony of life. Crossing the bridge we left the main road short of the town—to the keen disappointment of the men—and turned up what looked like a private drive through woods. After going about a mile and a half we came on a group of buildings which proved to be our destination for the night. It was dark and not easy to see much, and we accepted placidly a staff officer's information that the regiment's billeting area lay on the right side of a small stream. " You will find a farm—it was all I could do for you, but I expect you will all be able to get into it," he said. Tired and footsore as we were, we felt certain we should be able to fix ourselves up anywhere. The farm comprised three cottages, a large building and a huge haystack with a corrugated iron roof. We got most of the men on the hay under the corrugated iron roof. Of course, as soon as they lay down they pulled out cigarettes and pipes for a satisfying smoke after the long march. This made Goyle dance with fury, and he sent me up on top of the stack to have all the cigarettes put out. It seemed hard on the men, but he was quite right,

THE MOVE UP

as they would certainly have set the stack on fire.

Having got the men settled I went off to find the officers' quarters. These proved to be the two lower rooms of an empty house. There was no furniture in the house at all, simply a thick layer of straw on the floor. However, it had been a long march, and the straw looked inviting enough. I got my valise off the transport, unrolled it in a corner, took off my boots and coat and slid into my sleeping-bag. Others did the same in different corners of the room. The room was not very well lighted, and one or two late comers, who stepped on people's faces or feet in their efforts to find a corner for themselves, came in for a good deal of abuse. In a quarter of an hour we were all sound asleep. When we woke in the morning we took stock of our quarters, and found they were not so sumptuous as tired limbs and thankfulness to be able to stretch ourselves out rolled up in blankets had led us to suppose. For by daylight we could see by inscriptions scratched on the walls that the last occupants of the place had been a company of the —th Regiment of Turcos. We had been sleeping in what for a time had been a barracks for native troops. On going outside the building and taking a stroll we discovered a pretty little château which the officers of another regiment had annexed for their use. They had all slept in beds, washed in comfort, and were having breakfast on a smooth green lawn, surrounded by flowers. We had nowhere to have breakfast except by the side of a wall outside the Turcos' house, and we felt we had done badly over our billets. However, the etiquette of billeting gave the château to the other regiment who had first taken it, and we had to put up with what we had got.

The next night we set out on the march again. The march was twenty miles, and proved a severe task for the men after their long spell in the trenches, coming as it did on top of the eighteen-mile march of the night before. It is always the second or third march which tells most on men, and after the first dozen of our twenty miles they began to fall out, till there was a long string of stragglers behind the brigade. In vain the company officers tried to keep their companies together, nothing could make the weary, footsore men

THE MOVE UP 79

keep their fours. Tired as some of the officers were themselves, it was a heavy strain passing up and down the company, stopping to issue "falling out" tickets and running on to catch up the column again. The hardest task of all fell to the subaltern who was detailed to bring up the rear party, and who was not allowed to come into billets until the last man was in. To this unfortunate officer fell the task of trudging along at half a mile an hour behind a group of dead-tired, limping, footsore men. He got into billets four hours after everybody else.

The officers' billets on this occasion were better than those of the night before, for we found a house which had been used by German officers when the town was in the enemy's hands. The house was large and comfortable, and belonged to the mayor of the town. It had been cleared of all valuables, but whether the mayor had done this himself before his departure, or the German officers had looted the place, I cannot say. From the look of things I should imagine that the mayor had taken away all he could and the Germans anything that was left. They had evidently broken open a writing-desk and some drawers, and scattered the contents all over the place. I was guilty of a little looting on my own account, as I found a tattered paper-covered copy of "Madame Bovary," and not having finished it when it was time to leave, slipped it in my haversack.

We again spent the day around the billets, and as we had a mail with a sack of parcels sent up with the ration convoy we had plenty to occupy ourselves. On active service washing is not necessarily done before breakfast. It is too elaborate a ceremony to be done in a hurry. First a complete outfit has to be got together; one may have a razor but no shaving-brush, or a piece of soap but no towel, or a hairbrush but no comb; possibly one has nothing at all, in which case one is treated as a general nuisance, and borrows from others with difficulty. But, as a rule, with a depleted cleaning outfit of, say, a razor, a comb and a bit of sponge, the rest can be collected and spread out on a towel. The toilet is then a leisurely process, after which, feeling very clean and fresh and superior, one strolls across to the mess van in one's shirtsleeves for a glass of

THE MOVE UP

vermouth and a cigarette. After washing there were the letters brought in by the mail to answer, and then lunch and a couple of hours' sleep.

At dusk we moved off again, this time for a very short march, for four miles brought us to our destination, and we were only moved on a little way in order to make room for other troops following on behind.

A night in the village and off we started once more. At one point we passed our Divisional General. From the cheery greeting one of his staff officers gave me I surmised something was on foot, and this conjecture proved right, for on reaching a town ten miles distant our billeting orders were suddenly cancelled, and we were told to go on another four miles and entrain. The remainder of the way led through the forest of Compiègne. It was a bright moonlight night, and the forest by night was incomparably lovely. With moonlight playing quietly through the branches it was hard to believe that the forest had ever held troops creeping from tree-trunk to tree-trunk seeking to take each other's lives. In the earlier days of the war we could imagine rival cavalry patrols stealing quietly towards each other along the grass-turfed, shady side of the broad white road, and many a small, bloody encounter must those old trees have seen.

We came on the siding where we were to entrain in a piece of open common. It took some manipulation to get forty men into each truck, but at last we all settled in, a bugle was blown, and we stole away towards the north.

VI. THE MOVE UP (2)

OUR train journey did not promise to be a comfortable one. We were three aside on the seats of the first-class carriage and the disposition of legs was not easy. However, we all slept without much difficulty, and for six hours the train rumbled through the night to the accompaniment of snores and grunts. The day broke gloriously, and when we looked out of the windows we found ourselves going through a lovely bit of France. Breakfast was the next question; we had in our ration-box a tin of jam, a loaf and a half of bread, and two tins of sardines, also a packet of cocoa. This last possession did not look as though it was going to be particularly useful, as we had nothing but cold water in our bottles. We ate the sardines and bread and jam and took one or two unappetizing sips from our water-bottles. Then the train stopped, and looking out of the window I saw one or two men standing beside the engine with canteens in their hands. They handed up their tins to the driver, who filled them with boiling water from an exhaust pipe and they proceeded to make tea. Borrowing a couple of canteens from the next carriage I took the packet of cocoa and followed the men's example, so our breakfast was complete.

About noon we reached our destination, a pretty cathedral town in Northern France. After waiting a little while in a siding we detrained and marched off. The town was evidently not one of those which the Germans had entered, for it looked prosperous and well filled. The same sense of security pervaded the country through which we marched; we were, in fact, outside the zone of war. After following a straight white road out of the town for some four miles, we came to a village where we were to billet for the night. The village priest came forward to assist us in billeting, and the squire of the place sent over a present of wine for the officers and put up the Colonel and Adjutant in his house.

The next morning I borrowed a horse and rode in to ——, the town at which we had detrained. I had got from the mess president a list of things wanted for the officers' mess

THE MOVE UP 85

and proceeded to shop. Two dozen eggs were among the items on the list, and I had an opportunity of buying these from a farm cart in one of the streets leading to the town. A passer-by happened to overhear me making the bargain and upbraided the good woman selling me the eggs for charging too high a price. I could not quite follow the conversation, which took place in animated French, but I gathered that to ask a British soldier so much for eggs was no way for an ally to behave to a guest and brother-in-arms, and that the farmer's wife thought that passers-by should mind their own business.

This sense of hospitality which the passer-by had shown pervaded all my shopping transactions ; the tradespeople were all cordial, obliging, and most moderate in their charges.

I lunched at the main hotel of the town, which was filled with all the nondescript and various personages who follow an army ; there were gentlemen chauffeurs, Red Cross workers, interpreters, and one or two staff officials. At my table there was a clean-shaven, shrewd-looking man wearing the red tabs of staff, who spoke with a strong cockney accent, and did not give the impression of having been a soldier all his life. He said he was attached to general headquarters as spy officer, that is to say, he was responsible for discovering any espionage which went on in our lines. In civil life he looked as though he might be one of those private inquiry agents who advertise in the columns of the Press that they are ready to undertake divorce, financial, and other investigations of a confidential nature. I dare say this is what he was, and I am sure he was a very capable man for the position he held.

After lunch I had my hair cut and shampooed. It was delightful to sit in a hairdresser's chair again and taste some of the luxuries of civilization. I could not help envying the barber his peaceful occupation, which I dare say he is still pursuing and which I knew he would be doing long after I was out of reach of a machine brush and hair oil; and I thought, too, how much pleasanter it would be to be attached to headquarters staff as an espionage officer and have one's lunch in the restaurant of a hotel instead of eating bully and biscuits and dodging shells in a ditch. However, it was no good reflecting and becoming discontented with one's lot, and after completing my pur-

THE MOVE UP

chases I rode back to the village where the regiment was billeted.

Our last march was the longest of all, as we marched all through the night and did not get into the billets where we were to sleep till dawn the next morning. Evans and I shared a room in a cottage, and after eating some breakfast with some delicious coffee, which the woman the cottage belonged to made us, we flung ourselves down on mattresses on the floor and slept. It was past two when I woke, and I hurried off to the headquarters mess to see if there was any lunch left. Luckily the mess sergeant had kept some of the stew he had made for lunch and heated it up for me. After putting down this and half a bottle of wine, I made my way back to the cottage. A stretch of mossy grass under a shady tree looked inviting, and flinging myself down I was soon asleep again.

Some providence must have been watching over me that day, for I woke just ten minutes before the regiment marched off. No one had been able to find me when the order came to move, and they had decided to go off without me. I was glad I had just woken in time, for an officer does not look at his best chasing after a regiment by himself down a road because he has been asleep.

I joined up the group of officers who were sitting by the mess van making a hasty tea and stuffing their haversacks with biscuits.

" I should advise you to take some food," said the Adjutant to me, " this may be your last chance. We are going to march five miles, load up on motor-buses, and the transport is to be left behind."

" *The transport to be left behind?* " some one echoed.

" Yes," the Adjutant answered a little grimly. " We're for it again."

When a regiment parts with its transport it generally means it is going to fight. We had been with our transport for so many days now that it came as quite a thrill to hear we were to leave it behind. A feeling half of relief that we were going on with the business and half of apprehension came over me.

We marched for an hour or so; at seven o'clock we reached the point of rendezvous for the motor-buses, a long straight stretch of road running through open country just beyond a

THE MOVE UP 89

village. Just before we got to the point of rendezvous the regiment was divided up into parties of thirty men, and a gap of twenty yards left between each party. We did this on the march so that no time was lost in sorting out the different parties. When the last division had been made and all the proper distances between parties obtained, the leading party halted and the others halted behind. The men were then cleared to the right side of the road so that the fleet of motor-buses could come and each halt opposite its party, load up, and move off again with the whole regiment stowed away in no longer time than it took to load thirty men.

When we got to the rendezvous there were no motor-buses and we had to wait. The nights were turning cold; however, not knowing when the next chance might come, most of the men prepared to sleep. In the rush to get off at the start, I had left my greatcoat with the transport and had only a Burberry and a woollen waistcoat with me. I undid my Burberry, unrolled it, pulled out the waistcoat and put both on. Then I lay down by the side of the road, taking care to have a stout tree between myself and any possible motor-cars—a very wise precaution if one is sleeping by the roadside anywhere near the Front—slipped my haversack under my head and went to sleep. A haversack makes quite a good pillow, and when one is tired any piece of ground, which enables one to lie on one's back and take the weight off one's feet, seems soft, and I was soon asleep. Not for long though, as after half an hour I woke with icy feet. I stamped about to warm them, but the thought of going to sleep again and waking up in another half-hour for the same reason was tiresome, so I cast my eye round in the night for some means of keeping warm. I saw what looked like a stack and going up found it was so. While I was busy pulling hay out of the side to make a bed, the motor-buses arrived, and we proceeded to embark. Having got all the men into my bus I was climbing up by the driver on his seat when he shook his head and pointed to the interior of the vehicle, which was a seething mass of Tommies. I shook my head over this and it looked like an *impasse*, as the other officers were all being made to get inside by the different drivers. However, a

THE MOVE UP 91

knowledge of French and of the ready response of the Frenchman to geniality saved me. For, while pretending to agree to go inside I stood talking with him while we waited to start, offered him a cigarette, and asked him about his wife and family, with the result that when we did set off he said, "*Montez, monsieur*," and made room for me on the seat beside him. He said that every night he was driving troops from one part of the line or another—French troops generally, and it was interesting to hear the way in which the French troops used the motor-buses. The warmth of the engine having reached my feet I fell asleep and nodded and lurched beside him on the seat blissfully unconscious for I don't know how many hours and miles. Once on the journey we halted for a quarter of an hour in a small village. The driver got off the bus and disappeared. Presently he came back and beckoned to me to come with him. I followed him into a cottage where he and several other drivers had had prepared against their arrival hot coffee and rolls of bread and butter. It was extremely kind of the man to have let me in for this feast, which was quite a private affair, and I have seldom enjoyed a cup of coffee more. On we went again and off I went to sleep once more At last, as day broke, we came to the village where we were to halt, climbed off the buses, and sat down by the roadside watching them roll away the way we had come to get more troops.

As we sat by the roadside we soon saw we were nearing more lively parts, for streams of refugees poured by all the time, flying in front of the advancing Germans who were pouring down in strength after the fall of Antwerp. We sat watching the refugees in silence. So this, then, was the reason for our leaving the Aisne and our long secretive seven days move.

VII. NEARING THE FIRING-LINE

"WE shall have a scrap to-day," said the Staff Captain.

"What makes you think so—heard anything?" I asked.

"No, but it is a Sunday, and a fresh batch of officers has arrived," he answered.

Up till then the worst fights in which the regiment had been engaged had always been on a Sunday or just after fresh officers had arrived with reinforcements. The regiment was, at the moment when the Staff Captain spoke to me, leading the brigade in column of route along a road which we knew ran in the direction of Germany. More than that we knew nothing. We had been on the move for the last few days. Where to or for what purpose we had no idea. All we knew was that in the middle of one night we had been roused from our billets where we were resting, and marched off in a northerly direction. We had marched by night and rested by day in different villages.

Never once was any definite information given us as to what was on foot.

Now, at last, if the Staff Captain's words were true, the move was coming to an end, and we were going into action. Well, if it had to be it had to be, and I think every man was ready to do what was required of him. The officers and draft who had joined us fresh from England were eager for their chance, but the others who had already had a good measure of fighting, and some of whom had been at Mons and on the Marne and Aisne, had not been sorry for the respite which the past fortnight had given. It had been a rest to be away from the sound of gun and rifle fire and go to sleep knowing the enemy was nowhere near, and that one had anyhow the whole of the next day to live.

However, as we marched along there were certain signs which told us that now this state of peace was over. Refugees began to pass us on the road—old men, farmers, and their wives and serving women. They looked scared, and had few possessions with them. We gathered from them that the Germans were somewhere ahead, pressing forward in vast numbers.

NEARING THE FIRING-LINE 95

Though we did not know it then, it was one of the fierce thrusts for Calais we were being sent to meet.

Further along we were halted in the straggling street of a town. The halt lasted more than the regulation ten minutes, and as we were wondering what was the cause of the delay a troop of British cavalry clattered through. A subaltern rode at the head of the troop, map in hand, hat jauntily over one ear. Presently the remainder of a cavalry brigade came by, and we knew then that the enemy must be somewhere near and that the cavalry were being sent out to get in touch with them.

They made a brave sight, those cavalrymen, clattering out to pave the way for the infantry, and I could not help envying them the excitement and uncertainty of their job.

By the time we advanced the enemy's position would be known and we should be just pawns pushed out at the will of a general to be taken or take.

When the cavalry had gone by we continued our march until we reached a point which was evidently as far as we were to go that evening. Here the Colonel sent for officers commanding companies and told them that his orders were to put out two companies on outpost duty along the banks of a canal and keep two in reserve with him in a farm building. It was the lot of my company to be one of the two on outpost duty.

Going out on outpost duty in the middle of a march is one of the hardest lots that can fall on an infantryman. It means that instead of being able to take his boots off, soap his feet (if they are sore), change his socks, have a dinner of hot stew and a good cup of strong tea, he has to spend the night out in the cold watching over the safety of those who are doing these delightful things. He may get a bit of sleep if he is not on group sentry, but it won't be with the same sense of security, and he must lie down in his heavy equipment and have his rifle under his arm.

Off we started with a regretful glance at the farm and others going to billet there in a cosy barn and cook themselves dinner at the kitchen fire. We soon came to the canal which was to form our outpost line. It lay about half a mile away and looked a very good object to have between ourselves and the enemy. There was

NEARING THE FIRING-LINE 97

one bridge, at which Goyle placed his Maxim. The men he lined along a bank about ten feet high which ran above the tow-path on our side of the canal. This bank proved a blessing in many ways. It saved the men the trouble of entrenching—one of the most irksome items of outpost duty after a long day's march—and provided cover behind which they could walk about, and even enabled them with great care to light small fires to cook tea over until darkness set in. But the bank might also— as Goyle, who had had experience of canal banks at Mons, pointed out—prove a death-trap in the morning, for it would provide a fine mark for the enemy's guns should they get on to it. He therefore insisted on each man scraping himself out a small bomb-proof shelter from under the bank.

By great good fortune, just behind the section for which my platoon was responsible, there was a cottage. The owners, an old man and his wife, came to the door when I knocked. Like so many of the French peasants they preferred to remain in their home in spite of the proximity of war. They were quite pleased to see Evans, my fellow-subaltern, and myself, and the old woman made us some most delicious coffee, boiled us four eggs, and gave us a loaf of bread. She was delighted with the five francs we were able to scrape up, and promised to get us breakfast in the morning.

It was dark when we had finished, and after a look along the lines, I rolled myself up in a quilt, which I had borrowed from the cottage, and with some straw under me went sound asleep on top of the bank. Not a shot was fired during the night or at dawn to disturb us, so that that night on outpost duty was one of unusual peace and comfort.

In the morning we packed up and continued our march. As we marched in fours along the road, I gathered that my suspicion that there had been really nothing in front of us was correct. A mile or two from the canal a regiment of Spahis passed us. Incredible as it may seem, these fine little fellows go to war in the scarlet cloaks in which they are dressed in time of peace. They are the most picturesque troops I have ever seen, with their mettlesome Arab horses, turbans, and sweeping scarlet cloaks fastened across the breast high up to the chin.

NEARING THE FIRING-LINE 99

Farther on we passed a more forceful sight of war. It was a tiny cavalry ambulance convoy. Just one hooded Red Cross wagon, driven by a blue-coated cavalryman and followed by a cuirassier with bandaged head, riding one horse and leading another with an empty saddle. What a picture that little convoy would have made if some artist could have caught it—the pathetic little wagon with its hidden load of pain, the charger and empty saddle, and the splendid cuirassier with the bandaged head sitting his horse for all the world to see, proud as a lover who has fought for his mistress.

A mile more and our march was done. We were halted by a wayside inn and told to eat our rations. I went into the inn to see if there was any prospect of a drink, but they were sold out of everything except coffee. That day was probably the briskest day's trade the little inn ever did, and looking at it now it seems odd that the landlady and her daughter should have been bustling about intent solely on business within what proved to be actually half a mile of the firing-line. Two hours later our guns were opening fire in a field by the inn on some Germans in the next village.

As we sat there we now saw two regiments of Cuirassiers retiring over the open ground towards us. They were part of a French cavalry division which had been lent to co-operate with the British. Magnificent-looking fellows they were, too, with their breastplates and long black plumes; the officers actually had their breastplates burnished, and looked just like our Life Guards at Whitehall.

When we had eaten our rations we fell in again and moved off, and a few hundred yards down the road came on our cavalry, dismounted behind some buildings. From them we learnt that the enemy had been located about half a mile farther down the road. We were told from this point to leave the road and move in sections across country, and in this formation passed on beyond the cavalry. They had done their job and found the enemy, and it was now for us to come and take up the line.

VIII. GETTING INTO ACTION

AFTER the cavalry had withdrawn my regiment was lined out along a road running at right angles to the road down which we had advanced. From this time onwards for the next ten days I only knew what the companies on my left and right were doing, and not always that. As a platoon commander, I was responsible for the fifty men under me, and all the information it was necessary for me to have was included in the orders which Goyle, my company commander, gave for the movements of my platoon. Therefore, for general knowledge of the battle, I had to rely on such deductions as I could make from sound of firing on my right and left and any gossip I could pick up when I went back to regimental headquarters.

Advancing to attack in these days of modern warfare is a very slow business. It is essential that platoons, companies, and regiments should move forward together in one line and not allow gaps to come between them, and what with one regiment waiting for another to advance, and each waiting for orders from their respective colonels, who in turn are waiting for the word from the Brigadier, there is often considerable delay. This delay is to a certain extent mitigated by the general policy of junior officers of pushing forward on their own initiative until they are stopped.

As a platoon commander one works with the platoon commander on one's left or right, leaving the platoon sergeant to keep in touch with the platoon on the other flank. To have a fellow subaltern to talk to as one lies in a ditch being shelled is a great comfort.

However, we were kept along the road we had first lined for about an hour before any further move was made, and most of the officers of the regiment congregated in a little group while we were waiting for orders. I was much interested in watching the doings of some gunner officers who had come up. Two of them were surveying the ground in front through field-glasses. From where we were we could see nothing, and as there had not been a shot fired that day we did not know how many of the enemy there were in front of us

GETTING INTO ACTION 103

or where they were. However, the gunners were able to see something, for, after a bit, they conferred with the battery commander. Acting on their information he sent back a message for the guns to come up, and up they dashed, wheeled into line in the field, and unlimbered.

I happened to be standing near the battery commander, and ventured to ask him what he was going to do.

" I'm going to shell ——ville," he replied.

He was a squat, stumpy little major, who looked as though he had just made a capital breakfast, and he spoke of his intentions with as much complacency as if he was going out for a morning's partridge-shooting. Two minutes later he had given a crisp order, and the six businesslike grey nozzles had barked in sharp succession, and sent six shells screaming over the quiet countryside. Poor——ville! Many shells have since crashed into the pretty little French village, but I shall never forget seeing its baptism of fire or the complacent way in which the tubby little major announced that he was going to shell the place.

Soon after this orders came for the infantry to advance, and Goyle sent for his four platoon commanders and gave his orders. Our company was responsible for keeping touch with the Dorchester Regiment on our left ; No. 5 platoon, under Evans, was immediately responsible for this, with No 6 (mine) next, and 7 (under Edwards), and 8 (under Mayne), on the right. This was to be the first day's fighting for Edwards and Mayne, as they had only come out from England with reinforcements two days before. Edwards had been a Sandhurst cadet a month ago, but Mayne was a retired officer who had fought in South Africa ; however, there was nothing to choose in composure between the boy and the man.

Goyle took us to a point where we could see the ground we were to move over, and showed us a ditch which he wished us to crawl along until we reached another ditch at right angles to it which we were to line. In this way we should be able to do the first part of the advance without being seen at all. Evans took his platoon out first, and when he had got a good start I followed with mine. He reached the ditch without mishap, but here we had to remain some while, as the Dor-

GETTING INTO ACTION 105

chester Regiment on our left had not got up in line with us. Verbal messages then passed between Evans and the subaltern in command of the right platoon of the Dorchester Regiment. Evans wanted to know why the Dorchesters were not in line with him, and the subaltern of the Dorchester's why he, Evans, had advanced so far. Up till now our guns behind had been firing steadily over our heads, and not a sound or sign had come from the enemy, but now suddenly, in the middle of the argument between Evans and the Dorchester subaltern, there was a different whistle in the air, a crash, and a white puff of smoke just behind us.

"Hullo!" Evans looked round and slid quickly to the bottom of the ditch.

The enemy's first shell was followed by two others, which burst about the same place, and then by three which fell farther over us.

"They are after our guns," said Evans.

This was my first taste of hostile shell-fire, but the shells passed so harmlessly overhead that it hardly seemed as though we were under fire at all. After a while orders came for us to continue our advance. This time my platoon had to lead the way and advance up a ditch to another parallel ditch about three hundred yards away. We gained the ditch without incident, but it was a queer experience, pushing forward over the empty fields, never knowing when we were coming on the enemy or what lay ahead of us. When my platoon and the platoon under Evans were safely in the ditch, No. 7 was told to follow. To reach our line No. 7 had to cross over some open ground, and this proved their undoing, for midway across a shell burst just in front of them, followed by another and another.

" By Jove," said Evans, " Edward's lot has been spotted."

We watched. Edwards, as soon as he came under fire, had halted his men beneath a bit of bank, and from where we were we could see no sign of a man above the surface of the ground. But the enemy battery had evidently found their mark, for they plastered the little bank with shrapnel. I watched, able to do nothing and sorry in my heart. It was a very fierce baptism of fire for a Sandhurst cadet, and I wondered how the boy was faring.

GETTING INTO ACTION 107

It was now well on towards dusk, and as the light failed the firing stopped. Slowly, what was left of the exposed platoon began to creep up to our ditch, and much to my delight Edwards himself came up unhurt with the first man. He said he had had ten men hit, a man sitting beside him killed, and a tree just above blown in half. The boy seemed none the worse for his experience, and only a little anxious lest he had exposed his men unnecessarily to fire.

It now looked as though we were to spend the night where we were. I posted a patrol out in some bushes ahead and told the men to get to work with their entrenching tools to improve their cover. As it grew darker, the strain of looking out into the night for an enemy who never appeared became oppressive. Evans reported from the left that he could see no sign of the Dorchester Regiment, and we appeared to be in rather an isolated position. Much to my relief Goyle came up soon and said he intended to withdraw the company to the place whence we had started. It was a great relief to be able to lie down close to our own guns and near the Colonel and regimental headquarters. As soon as the men were settled I went back to the first-line transport to get the officers' rations for the next day. Goyle had given me the job of feeding the five officers in the company, leaving it to me to make arrangements for cooking where possible, and, when not, to see that each had a parcel of food to last him through the day. I found the regimental quartermaster-sergeant busy issuing rations to the different company orderly corporals. The work was being done in a barn by the light of a guttering candle. In a corner of the barn five of Edwards's platoon, who had come under the shrapnel fire, lay stretched out stiff and cold.

The quartermaster-sergeant saluted me cheerily and packed my ration-box with our rations, giving me a piece of bacon to divide between us, a wedge of cheese, fifteen army biscuits, a tin of jam, and three small tins of bully beef. With the box under one arm I started back for the company. On the way, having learnt from a sentry where regimental headquarters were, I just peeped in to see what was going on. After the day's work, there is often something to be picked up at regimental

GETTING INTO ACTION 109

headquarters in the way of a tot of whisky from a bottle sent down by the Brigadier, or a helping from a dixie of soup sent up by the master-cook. Young subalterns are not supposed to hang about waiting for these delicacies, but if they do push a hungry face round the door and hastily withdraw it a kindly colonel or adjutant will often ask them in. Having therefore located regimental headquarters as being in the kitchen of a farm, I tapped on the door and asked if anyone had seen Goyle.

" Yes," here he is, said the Colonel, and I saw my company commander's nose emerge from a steaming cup of coffee. Round the fire were the Colonel, Adjutant, scout and machine-gun officers, the doctor, Goyle, and two other company commanders. These little informal gatherings are held by most regiments when the day's work is done and the night is not going to be busy, and a great relief it is, too, to be able to laugh and see the funny side of things after the strain of an anxious day. At the first sound of firing they melt.

I was given a cup of coffee and wheedled a cigarette out of a scout officer, who had just had some sent out from England. After warming myself for a quarter of an hour I said goodnight and returned to the company across the field, taking with me a bundle of straw from the farmyard, which made a capital bed.

IX. AN ATTACK AT DAWN

I HAD not been sleeping long when I was awakened by a foot gently feeling the small of my back.

Looking up, I saw Evans standing over me.

"Goyle wants you," he said; "he is just down there." Evans pointed to a dark corner of the ditch in which the company was spending the night.

I got up from the pile of straw on which I was lying and followed him. Goyle was squatting on the ground with a map and an electric torch which he was shading under his greatcoat. He had just come back from battalion headquarters, where he had been to receive orders.

"We are going to attack at dawn," he began, as soon as his four platoon commanders were settled round him. "We are to gain the line ———," he indicated the points on the map which marked the position we were to capture. "The Dorchesters have orders to take ———ville"—he pointed to a village on our

left—" and the —th Brigade are to take ——"
—he pointed to another village marked on the right. "The attack begins as soon as it is light, which will be 5 A.M. I want you to see now that the platoons return their tools" (we had been digging earlier in the night), "that each man has his rations, and that twenty-five bandoliers of spare ammunition are carried per platoon. The mist will cover the first part of our advance, and there must be no firing until the order is given by me."

We went off to carry out the instructions given, and then lay down to wait for the dawn.

Perhaps Evans and the other platoon commanders slept. I don't know. I know only that for my part I did not. The thought that we were to attack at dawn dispelled any lingering sleepiness. I looked at my watch—3 A.M.—in an hour it would begin to grow light. How would the day end? What would be the fate of the attack? I wondered if Goyle was awake, and thought I would go down to him. I peeped down into the corner of the ditch where I knew he was lying. A dark form lay stretched at full length, and I heard a gentle snore. I lay down again.

AN ATTACK AT DAWN

After a while, looking out in the direction of the enemy, I saw a faint flush low in the sky. I watched. The flush swelled to a vast crimson glow. I woke Goyle. For a moment we looked at the day breaking blood-red over the fields across which we were to fight our way. Then we went, one either way along the ditch, rousing the men.

The men yawned, stretched themselves, and stood to arms. Their bayonets, which they always kept fixed during the night, glittered faintly in the early light. The crimson flush was broken now, and streaks of yellow and pure white shot the sky.

Goyle caught my arm.

Low on the horizon the crest of a yellow ball just showed above the trees. " The sun," he said.

CRASH! bang! CRASH! bang! bang! bang!

We listened as our guns behind opened the ceremony with a salvo. They fired fast for five or ten minutes.

"The Dorchesters are advancing on our left, sir"—the message was passed down to Goyle.

He signed for the company to advance. The men crawled up out of the ditch and pushed over the country in a thin line. Evans was on my left, with Edwards and No. 8 platoon commander on the right.

We advanced very slowly, with long pauses, lying flat on the ground waiting for orders to continue. Now the officer commanding the company on the right would send word to say he had reached such a point, and would C Company come up in line with him ? Now Evans passed along that we were getting ahead of the Dorchesters. The attack is a very slow and ticklish business in these days of modern firearms. All this while steady firing could be heard on the right as the —th Brigade swung round, and for about an hour there was sharp firing on the left, but in front of us not a shot was heard.

At last we gained a group of cottages on a road which marked the point we had been told to reach. There was still no sign of the enemy, and had it not been for the firing on the right and left we should have doubted his existence in the neighbourhood, so quiet and peaceful did the cottages look.

AN ATTACK AT DAWN

However, we heard afterwards that the brigade on the right had suffered heavily, and that the brisk firing on the left was the Dorchester Regiment under machine-gun fire from the village they had been told to take. It just happened to be our luck that day to have an uncontested piece of frontage to advance over.

A road ran through the group of houses and beyond a ploughed field. At the end of the ploughed field there was a hedge and ditch, which formed a natural trench facing the enemy. In spite of the apparent absence of the enemy Goyle refused to allow the men to loiter about along the road or in the farms and cottages, but ordered the company to line this ditch. As it turned out later it was well he did so.

As soon as I had seen my platoon lined along their section of the ditch I went back to a farm behind to explore. I found Jenkins, my soldier servant, there before me, busy searching the farm for breakfast. He had found half a dozen new-laid eggs in an outhouse, kindled a small fire in the farmyard, and was boiling the eggs in his canteen. He was not, strictly speaking, supposed to be doing this, but soldier servants are a privileged class, and Jenkins was the most tactful of servants. On my going up to him to see what he was doing he pointed to the eggs triumphantly and said they were for me. So instead of telling him to join the company at once in the ditch I stayed with him to watch them boil. I had not been in the farmyard two minutes when suddenly sharp firing broke out from the ditch. So we had found something in front of us at last. I dashed across the ploughed field to my platoon, leaving Jenkins, quite unperturbed, still watching the eggs. Reaching the ditch I flung myself down beside Evans, who was lying against the bank peering to the front through the hedge. We could see nothing; however, our fellows continued to fire furiously. For the first minute or two the firing was so hot that both Evans and I thought there must be something ahead of us. As it continued, though we could still see nothing, we crept along behind the men to try to find out what they were firing at. My platoon sergeant informed me that he thought the enemy were lining the corner of a wood 400 yards away.

AN ATTACK AT DAWN 117

He had seen one or two dodging in and out among the trees. However, as no reply was made to our fire, I ordered that no man was to fire unless he saw something, and gradually the line grew quiet again.

Suddenly there was a dull report from a distant point in front, and a shell whistled overhead. Looking back, I saw it strike the roof of the farm where I had left Jenkins. Poor Jenkins! I wondered if he was still cooking those eggs! However, I had no time to speculate on his fate, for the enemy, having located our position owing to our own rather unnecessarily agressive outburst of rifle fire, began to shell us. Round after round they sent crashing into the cottages and farms, and then, shortening their range, began to put shots just over our ditch. Well it was that Matley had made all the men get into the ditch from the beginning. It was a fine deep ditch, and few of the many thousands of shrapnel bullets found their mark. Soon after the shelling started it began to rain heavily. It was a weird experience lying there in the ditch with the rain pouring down on us from above and the shrapnel bullets crashing sideways like a leaden hailstorm through the hedge. The men pulled their waterproof sheets from their packs, and, spreading these over themselves, lay down in the ditch, smoking unconcernedly. Now and again a wounded man whose cover had not been sufficient would crawl by. One very fat lance-corporal I remember, puffing along on his hands and knees as fast as his rifle and pack would let him. He kept slipping, catching his pack in the branches, and swearing profusely. He had been caught in the most fleshy part of his body, and evidently was of the opinion that there was no place like home, for from time to time he grunted, " Stretcher bearer ! Stretcher bearer ! 'Ere ! I've been 'it ! " He was a most comic sight, and I couldn't help laughing as he passed.

The firing went on intermittently throughout the day. At dusk we were withdrawn, another company taking our place in the ditch. We were formed up behind the shelter of a farm wall on the road behind, and told we were going to be taken back into reserve for the night.

By the farm I found Mulligan, a brother

AN ATTACK AT DAWN 119

subaltern. Taking me gently by the elbow he led me into the farm kitchen, through a door beyond, and down some cellar steps. I lit my torch to look around. The cellar floor was heaped with broken and empty bottles and corks. On a shelf were half-finished glasses of wine. A party of German soldiers had evidently been in before us and helped themselves, breaking what they could not drink. However, they had left one or two bottles intact amid the debris, from which Mulligan and I each had a good glass of red wine, for which I hope the owner, if he ever returns to his battered home, will forgive us.

Coming out of the farm, much to my delight, I met Jenkins still alive, in spite of the shell-fire. He pressed two cold, hard objects into my hand.

" How did you get these ? " I asked.

" They were them eggs I was cooking this morning," he replied ; " I had to quit when that first shell came—nearly went up, eggs and all, with it. But I went back afterwards. The fire was out—but they was boiled all right, if you don't mind 'em hard."

X. THE RESERVE COMPANY

AFTER D Company had taken over our section of trench we remained on the road behind for a time, while the authorities were deciding what to do with us. Goyle said the question was whether we were required to fill a gap between our right company and the Dorchesters on our left or whether our right company and the Dorchesters between them could span this gap and enable us to go back as reserve company into billets.

We waited in the rain for our orders. The men stood expectantly with their rifles slung over their shoulders, their hands in their pockets, and their greatcoat collars turned up to their ears. They said little. Now and again one would say to another hopefully, " We're going back to billets—ain't we, Bill ? " One or two of my N.C.O.s came up and asked me if I knew what was going to happen, and I told them the situation, about which, like the dutiful fellows they were, they expressed no opinion. He is a wonderful fellow on

THE RESERVE COMPANY 121

active service is Tommy Atkins. However roughly his inclinations may be torn he never says a word, but just does what is required of him so long as he can stand. Those men would have gone off to fill the gap that night without a question or thought except that it had to be done, and perhaps a " Gor blimey ! " on life in general and European warfare in particular.

However, it was to be billets that night. Goyle came up with the order from battalion headquarters. The company fell-in in fours and marched down the road. I don't know what it is, but there is a sort of feeling about a body of men marching which conveys a lot to a trained ear. In the ready click of the rifle to the shoulder and the steady tramp of the fifty pairs of feet behind me I could read hearts full of thankfulness as we headed down the lane towards the tiny village where we were to billet.

It was by now nearly ten o'clock. The village itself consisted of two farms and half a dozen cottages, and the Adjutant was disposed to say that it was hardly worth billeting the men in view of the lateness of the hour and the possibility of their having to turn out at short notice. He suggested they should lie down in a field. However, Evans and I guaranteed to have all the men in billets within a quarter of an hour and to make ourselves personally responsible for knowing where they all were and turning them out at short notice if required. The Adjutant, who was merely taking up the point of view proper to adjutants of not wanting to run the risk of any company being caught napping, was agreeable to this, and off we started.

To be able to billet a company quickly is a question of practice. The eye quickly gets trained to know what amount of men will go into what space and the look of likely places. To stow away 200 men in a tiny village of two farms and four cottages would at first seem a difficult task, especially when a certain amount of the space has already been taken up by different details attached to battalion headquarters. Barns are the first things to look for, and we were lucky in finding two, which each held fifty men. The French barns always have plenty of straw in them, and make warm, snug lying. An empty stable took another

THE RESERVE COMPANY 123

fifty men, and an outhouse twenty-five ; the remaining twenty-five had to be content with a sort of porch which ran along a wall. These last we were subsequently able to transfer to the barn on finding there would just be room for them. The process of billeting the men did not take more than the quarter of an hour we had estimated, one of us going ahead to explore, the other following with the men and standing at the entrance to the barn or outhouse, counting them in and flashing his torch into the interior to show the way.

Having got the men under cover, we looked about for a place for ourselves. Goyle had been offered a mattress in the kitchen of the farm where the Colonel and Adjutant were making their battalion headquarters. He was also no doubt going to have some of the Colonel's supper, and might be considered arranged for for the night. But there was no room for four hungry subalterns at battalion headquarters. We had received our day's rations and were expected to look after ourselves. Four sergeants were using the kitchen of the other farm, and of the cottagers only one, from a light in the window, looked as though it was inhabited. Evans and I pushed our way into this but found the kitchen already occupied. Six Tommies were sitting round the stove watching a stew simmer in a pan. They did not belong to our company, but were some of the headquarters details. The cottage was certainly theirs by right of annexation, and Evans and I turned to go out.

"Beg pardin, sir," said one of the men; "but there's another room at the back." This was extremely kind and hospitable of the man, as the little class distinctions between officer and man are to a certain extent preserved on active service, and the Tommy who has found a nook likes to keep it to himself just as much as the officer.

Evans and I accepted the invitation and went to inspect the other room. We found a comfortable cottage bedroom with two large four-post beds. The old woman to whom the cottage belonged and her husband said we were welcome to the use of the beds, and the sight of them was so tempting that I am afraid we did not trouble to inquire where she and her old man would sleep.

Jenkins, my servant, and the other two

THE RESERVE COMPANY 125

platoon commanders being then found, we put a stew of bully beef and vegetables on the fire, and, having eaten this, doubled up on the two beds.

Impossible to describe the joy of throwing off our wet boots and coats, stretching ourselves on the mattresses, and pulling a blanket up to our chins. We were soon all fast asleep.

After six hours real rest we woke feeling fit for anything. When we went out into the lane we found Jenkins in the middle of preparations for breakfast. He had dragged a table outside the cottage, discovered two chairs and two packing-cases, and laid four places with a miscellaneous assortment of knives and forks. For breakfast we had some fried ration bacon, a small and carefully apportioned wedge of bread each from the only loaf to be found in the village, coffee, and a tin of marmalade.

The company passed the day in converting a ditch into a trench. Although they were supposed to be resting in reserve, the men needed no urging to dig. The day before they had come under shrapnel fire when they were fortunately in a fine natural trench, but the memory of the murderous hail of bullets which had swept over their heads was sufficiently vivid to make them all anxious to provide themselves with equally good cover against a second attack. Each man worked away individually for himself, digging away into and under the ground until he had scooped a little burrow in which he would be secure from shrapnel, no matter how accurately it burst over the trench. As the men finished their burrows to their satisfaction they lay down in them, pulled out their pipes and cigarettes, and smoked, watching with complacent interest the efforts of neighbours who had roots or rocks or other difficulties in the soil to contend with.

The morning passed quietly, but at noon the enemy sent several shells over the ground where we were. One of these shells struck one of the cottages, crumpling it like a matchbox. I happened at the time to be back in the cottage where we had slept, helping Jenkins to concoct a stew for lunch. It was pitiful to see the terror of the old peasant woman and her husband, who sat dumbly in their kitchen, waiting for one of the great projectiles to come and wreck their home. As each shell

THE RESERVE COMPANY 127

fell the old woman lifted her hands and gave a little pitiful gasp. It was all more than she could understand, and no efforts of Jenkins or myself could calm her. However, they were a brave old couple, and as soon as the shelling was over busied themselves getting us potatoes and carrots for our stew from a store they had in a loft. They were delighted with a tin of army bully beef which we gave them for themselves. Except for this old couple, the farms and cottages were deserted, and I rather wondered why they had remained. Probably because they were too frightened and bewildered to do anything else.

Just before dusk we heard the dull report of a heavy gun in the distance. *R-rump—* CRASH—a shell burst a quarter of a mile to our right. Again the gun boomed, and again the dull " *R-rump,*" followed by a loud explosion and cloud of mud and earth in the same place. The men stirred uneasily in their dug-outs. They knew what it was—60 lb. high-explosive melinite. It was no joke like shrapnel, this. If the enemy happened to turn a few on to us we should be blown to bits. It was an anxious time listening to the gun and waiting for the shells to explode. But they did not seem to be swinging round in our direction, and darkness found us all still safe. At eight the order came for the company to go back into the firing-line.

XI. A NIGHT ATTACK

AFTER twenty-four hours in reserve it was our turn to go back into the firing-line and relieve A Company. We took over A Company's trenches at dusk, Goyle going with each platoon commander, showing him his section, and giving orders about the posting of groups and improvement of cover.

My section of trench had already been worked on by the company we took over from. The officer before me had scooped out a dug-out for himself at one end and lined it with straw. This I marked off for my own use, and then went along the line to see that all the men were busy. By the time I had inspected the trench and put out an advanced post it was quite dark, and I settled myself down in my own dug-out with a pious hope that the night would remain fine and we should all be able to pass it comfortably. There was no sound from the front, and it looked as though we should be undisturbed. One by one the stars came out, the night grew colder, and I pulled on my greatcoat. It was weird lying there in the darkness, hearing nothing, seeing nothing, with only the dark shapes of the men on each side and the occasional tinkle of an entrenching tool against a stone to remind one that one was taking part in a great war. I wondered what my friends at home were doing, thought of dances at the Ritz and the happy days when one dressed for dinner, and smiled to think what a funny sight I must look tucked up for the night in a ditch.

As I lay there I heard far away on the right the sound of rifle fire. Were they our troops or the French ? Perhaps it was one of our divisions which we had been told was swinging round on our flank. So the division had done its march and was fighting now. I was glad we were not. It was much better to lie peacefully in a ditch. Fighting meant seeing one's pals killed—crawling about, peering forward with tired eyes—worry, anxiety, with, of course, always the fever of excitement. But we had all had a full share of excitement, and were not sorry to lie still until we were wanted. Hullo ! The sound of firing was drawing nearer and

A NIGHT ATTACK

swelling in volume. That must be the brigade on our right engaged. Ah! There were two sharp shots from the farm where the next company lay.

"Pass along the word for every man to stand to," I called, jumping to my feet.

"Sergeant X," I said to the N.C.O. next to me, "go down the trench and see that every man is awake."

Pht! pht! pht!

I ducked down into the trench. Half a dozen bullets came singing through the edge. There was sharp firing now on our right. The next company was evidently engaged. Away beyond the rifle fire had swelled into one big crash of sound. Suddenly a hot fire broke out in front of us. To the left I heard our two Maxims, like watchdogs, barking viciously. It was a night attack, then—the enemy had come up to have a go at us.

"Quick—get into the trench and line along to your left. Where do you want me?"

I looked up and saw Mulligan hurrying his men into my trench. He had been sent up with his platoon from the reserve company to strengthen the line.

"Anywhere you like, old boy," I called back; "but I should get down out of that quick." The bullets were literally singing round him.

Our men were now all standing up to the parapet, firing into the night. I craned forward, trying to see in the darkness. A bullet lopped a branch off my ear, and I withdrew my head hurriedly.

"They're all awake, sir," said Sergeant X, as he returned to his place beside me.

"So it seems," I answered, as the din from our rifles swelled into a deafening volume. "Here, mind where you are pointing that gun," I said to the man on my left, as he brought down a bit of the hedge in front of my nose in his effort to get off five rounds in as many seconds.

"No. 5 platoon are running short of ammunition," the word came down the trench.

"Tell No. 6 to pass along any they have to spare and save their fire as much as possible," I ordered.

It was going to be a tight business this, with the enemy's fire growing hotter every minute and our ammunition supply running short.

Again the message came down, "No. 5 platoon are running short of ammunition."

A NIGHT ATTACK

I looked at Sergeant X. We had already sent men back for fresh supplies.

"I'll go back, sir," said Sergeant X. It seemed impossible for him to get out of the trench and cross the bullet-swept open ground. Still, it was the only thing to be done. I nodded.

Grasping his rifle, he turned to clamber out of the trench. Just as he was going a voice from behind called, "Where will you have this, sir?"

There was a thump behind, and two men rolled over into the trench dragging a box of ammunition after them. They sat up and mopped their foreheads. "Lord! it's like hail out there," said one of them breathlessly, "and that stuff weighs about a ton," pointing to the box of ammunition.

"Well, come on, mate," and back they went out of the trench to the rear for more.

Sergeant X and I wrenched the lid off the box of ammunition and started passing the bandoliers down the trench.

"Pass these right along to No. 5 platoon," I ordered.

A second box was brought up by two more

panting men. I distributed the contents among my own platoon. This put a better complexion on things. With plenty of ammunition we had nothing to fear, but the anxiety had been great. The sensation of running short of water in the desert is as nothing compared to that of running short of ammunition in action.

"They're getting closer, aren't they?" I said to Sergeant X, listening to the enemy's fire.

"I think they are, sir." He refilled his magazine and bent once more over the rifle.

"By gad! did you see that flash—they are only a hundred yards off. Here, give me that." I took the rifle from a man next me who had been wounded, and laid it, with the bayonet fixed, on the parapet in front. At the same time I drew my revolver and put it ready for use by my other hand. It was getting exciting this—quite pleasantly so.

"What do we do if they charge—get out and meet 'em?" I asked. My sergeant had had more experience of action than I, and I felt I could well afford to ask his advice.

"Just stay where we are, sir," he answered; "but they won't do that; they don't like

A NIGHT ATTACK 135

these "—he tapped his bayonet. He was a splendidly calm fellow, that sergeant, and it was good to feel him firm as a rock beside me. All men, N.C.O.s, officers, and privates, instinctively lean towards each other when the corner is tight.

For the next five hours the firing continued, sometimes dying down, sometimes swelling to a sharp volley. Ammunition boxes arrived and were emptied. There were moments of acute anxiety when the supply seemed running short. Each man was told to keep fifteen rounds by him at all costs to meet a charge. Sergeant X bent steadily over his rifle, pumping lead into the dark patch where the enemy appeared to be. Sometimes I could hear guttural voices and harsh words of command, somewhere away there in the blackness the enemy were lying. I could see clearly for about forty yards. Would masses of dark shapes suddenly appear? They should have ten rounds from the rifle, then six from the revolver, and then the bayonet would be left. Furtively under cover of the parapet I lit a cigarette, and holding it well screened from the front, puffed big satisfying gasps. All the while the rifles rattled like the sharp ticking of a clock.

The firing grew quieter, and from the front there was now only an occasional shot. I suddenly felt sleepy, as though lulled by the rattle of the rifle fire. I sat down a moment on the edge of my dug-out.

"Mr. Mulligan's compliments, and could you tell him the time, sir?" I pulled myself together with a start. By Jove, I had nearly been asleep. "What's the time, sergeant?" I asked. There was no reply. Sergeant X was nodding as he stood, arms folded over his rifle. He, too, as the firing died down had been overcome by sleep. I sent back the time to Mulligan, each man passing the message to the man next him.

"Mr. Mulligan's compliments, and would you like a biscuit, sir?" A biscuit was pressed into my hand which had come the same way as the message.

"Mr. ——'s compliments to Mr. Mulligan, and would he care for a piece of cheese?" I wrapped a piece of cheese in a piece of paper and sent it back.

So we kept passing messages to one another

A NIGHT ATTACK

all through the night, and no man slept. With the enemy a hundred yards away it was advisable they should not; but, like Sergeant X and myself, each, once the fierce strain of firing had passed, found the inclination wellnigh irresistible.

At last the dawn broke, and we saw the ground clear in front of us.

XII. THE FARM IN THE FIRING-LINE

A FARM lay behind our trench. Just in front of the farm there ran a wooden fence. This fence had been loopholed and banked with earth, and was now held by a platoon of infantry. Trenches ran to the right and left in continuation of the fence, and were manned by the remaining platoons of the company. For two days now the enemy had attacked the farm, and all through the past night bullets had come smack-smack against the walls, like heavy hailstones. It was a fair-sized farm built round a yard, three sides grain lofts and cattle sheds and the remaining side a dwelling-place. The company commander, the company sergeant-major, the stretcher-bearers, and others who were attached to company headquarters were standing about in the yard. One or two of the men had their coats off and were shaving and washing in buckets of water.

As there had been no firing since dawn, and

FARM IN THE FIRING-LINE 139

the enemy had evidently withdrawn after their unsuccessful attack during the night, Evans and I left our platoons and came into the farm.

Goyle, like the wise company commander he was, made no comment on our having left our trenches, relying on us to know when we ought to go back, and said that there was a room in the farm which the farmer's wife had set apart for the officers, and that we should find some food inside. This room, which was evidently the best parlour, was approached through the kitchen which opened on the front door.

Never shall I forget the sight as I opened the front door and looked into the kitchen. The small stone-flagged room was filled with civilians. These were evidently peasants from outlying cottages who had left their homes when the fighting began and flocked to the farm as a central place of refuge. At a wooden table sat a party of four women, two with children. One woman was weeping bitterly. The others were trying to console her. All were drinking from bowls of soup. The farmer's wife was stirring a fresh pot of soup over the stove.

She was a fine-looking woman, with proud, sad eyes. Seeing Evans and me standing at the door, she beckoned to us to come in, and gave us each a cup of soup. Beside the stove sat an old, old man, his head resting against his hand, staring fixedly before him.

Sometimes he moaned gently. He sat like this all day, refusing to talk to anybody, or to eat anything, or to be comforted. The farmer's wife told us that the day before a shell had hit his cottage and killed his horse. He was the village carrier. The horse was perhaps as old as himself—as horses' years are measured—still it had been his companion and means of livelihood, and now it was taken from him. He could not understand it all—why the shell had come to wreck his home and kill his horse. He just sat there moaning and staring before him. We turned away. Neither we nor the farmer's wife could do anything. But with the weeping woman at the table it might be different. The farmer's wife thought that we, being British officers, could do something. She brought the woman up to us and she told us her tale. Her husband, it seemed, had been hit by a bullet while working in his field. He now lay

FARM IN THE FIRING-LINE 141

out there wounded. She could not say she was sure if he was dead, but could we go and get him in. They had fired at her when she tried to go out to him. It was terrible to feel he was still lying there. We asked where the field was and then looked at each other helplessly. It lay in no man's land, between ours and the German lines. Perhaps at night, but for the rest of the day, no—we could do nothing. While we were drinking our soup two more refugees came in: a broken-looking middle-aged peasant, with red-rimmed eyes and thin shambling legs, and his wife. He was clinging round his wife's neck, tears pouring from the red-rimmed eyes. He, too, like the old peasant by the stove, was speechless; his wife told us that the Germans had taken him and made him march in front of them for three days.

She repeated the words "*trois jours*," her voice shaking with passion. The farmer's wife set the couple at the table and gave them soup from the pot. I wondered that she, too, did not join in the general weeping; but she went quietly and sadly about her work, saying little, giving food and drink to the afflicted people who had come to her kitchen, tending her pots and pans and fire. She asked no questions about the enemy, where they were or when we should drive them from the farm. She showed no signs of the night of terror she must have passed as the fight raged about her house. It was as though she stood for the spirit of France, proud to suffer for her country, confident in the prowess of her men, and patient and undoubting that they would succeed.

Later, when Goyle came, she ushered us all into the parlour she had reserved for our use. She watched us for a moment as we opened a tin of bully beef and pulled some biscuits from our pockets, and then, motioning to us to put these things away, began to dust the table and lay a cloth. In a short while she had put before us a dainty lunch, soup, boiled chicken, a stew of vegetables, coffee, and cheese. We would have preferred our servants to have done the cooking and waited on ourselves, so that she could look after her own people, but she insisted on doing everything herself, bringing each dish in. We asked her if we could do anything for her, and she drew up a methodical list of things she wanted from a neighbouring village—coffee, rice, flour, and oil for her lamp.

FARM IN THE FIRING-LINE 143

I got up to get these things, and at the door she stopped me and pressed her well-worn purse into my hand to buy the things. I had difficulty in making her take the money back.

Outside the farm I found a party of men burying one of the company who had been killed in the night. They had wrapped him in his coat, and were digging a rough grave by the roadside. One of the men was at work on a wooden cross made of two bits of board from the lid of a ration-box. He had scrawled R.I.P. and the date in large letters, and was laboriously tracing out the dead man's name and number.

The village where I was to get the provisions lay about half a mile away along an open, desolate road. All along the road men lay entrenched. The word had gone round that the enemy had withdrawn, and most of the men were sleeping beside their rifles. Some of the inhabitants of the village were coming back after the attack, and I found a tiny store open where I could get the things the farmer's wife required. On my way back I passed a wine shop, which was crowded with peasants, all talking and drinking coffee and little glasses of rum.

I wondered what they thought of it all, and imagined they were too bewildered to have any opinions. On all their faces were evident signs of satisfaction at being able to return to the village. They thought that the "*boches*" were by now probably running back hard to Germany, and all would be over in a few days.

As I stood in the doorway three civilian youths approached, two of them supporting a third between them. The lad in the middle looked white and scarcely able to stand. I went up to see if I could do anything. The two with him told me that they had found the boy lying in a field; he had been hit in five places by shrapnel. They thought he must have been lying there unattended for three days. The boy himself watched me with dumb, pain-ridden eyes. Very weakly and slowly he raised his hand to his mouth and pointed to his tongue, which was black and swollen. "*Soif*," he whispered. Of course, he had had no water all the time. I had him taken into a cottage and laid on a table. I got a glass of water from a well and held it to his

FARM IN THE FIRING-LINE 145

lips. He was too weak to raise his head, but his friends supported him, and he drank the water slowly and steadily. As he drank a little smile played about his lips, and when the glass was empty, before they laid him down, he nodded his head and smiled at me as only those smile for whom one has done some last service and whose life is nearly done.

I made my way back to the farm with sickness in my heart. Not all the fighting nor the strain of war had affected me as the sight of those suffering, helpless people whose ground we were using for our battlefield.

That night we said good-bye to the farmer's wife and pushed on beyond the farm. We were all happy to feel we were leaving her behind the security of our lines. As she stood at the door and watched us go there was still the same look in her eyes as when we came—a look of sadness, resignation, and infinite courage.

XIII. PUSHING FORWARD

AN hour before dawn the men stood to their arms in the trenches, but as the daylight grew and there was no sound or sight of the enemy, first one man and then another got out of the trench. These being allowed to walk about with impunity the others soon followed their example. Fires were lit for cooking, and men spread themselves on the ground behind the trench reading old copies of newspapers, or mending their clothes, or cleaning their rifles. Here and there parties could be seen carrying away corpses which had been stiff and cold behind the trench for the last forty-eight hours. Goyle, my company commander, walked across from his headquarters. The day before it had been impossible for him to get to us, and messages were brought by orderlies, who crawled up on their stomachs along a narrow ditch.

"Morning," said Goyle; "looks as though they had cleared."

PUSHING FORWARD

"Yes, sir," I answered, "there has been no sign of anything ahead this morning."

"I reckon that was their transport we heard, sir—they was rumbling along a road there, sir, all the night," said my platoon-sergeant.

The man was probably right, for all through the night a rumbling of wagons had been plainly audible along a road behind the enemy's lines. The night before we had been attacked fiercely, but though they had come very near us they had not been able to break through. During the day the enemy had remained quiet, contenting themselves with sniping, and now evidently, under cover of darkness, they had withdrawn to another position.

"Well, I suppose we shall push on now," I said to Goyle.

"Yes, I expect so," he answered.

Our orders to advance came at four o'clock. Goyle came down to give the necessary instructions to platoon commanders. We were to push forward straight to our front, keeping under cover as much as possible. He said he believed that the ground was all clear in front of us, but that it would be as well to take precautions.

Evans and I therefore led our platoons down a ditch which led direct to the front. We eventually came out by a large farm building which a day or two ago had been in the hands of the Germans. It had been known to the British troops as " the hospital," because the Germans had hoisted a Red Cross flag on a pole on the roof. But " the hospital " had also been used by the enemy as an observing station, and our guns had been obliged to shell it on two or three occasions. We examined the building with interest. The place was evidently a dairy farm on a large scale, for three sides were cowsheds, and there was a big store of hay. At the far end was the dwelling-house, over which the Red Cross had been hoisted. The place had perhaps been used as a hospital, for in the bottom room we found a long riding boot, which had been cut off a wounded man, and a blood-soaked pair of the well-known blue-grey breeches. However, on going up on to the roof we found the facilities for seeing over our lines so remarkable that the shells from our guns were evidently justly placed.

I made the tour of the farm with the doctor

PUSHING FORWARD

of the Dorchesters, who was thinking of taking it over as a hospital himself. When we came down from the roof we found two farm girls outside. They asked us anxiously if it would be safe for them to stay there that night, and we assured them it would. They said they had gone off a mile or two for two or three days, but now they had come back to look after the cows. They were a pair of very cool young ladies, who seemed to regard the German occupation of their farm as no more than a heavy rainstorm, to be avoided while it lasted, but not to be worried about once it was over. The doctor and I went round to look at the cowsheds. The beasts were all in their stalls, some evidently suffering a good deal from want of milking. In the first shed we came to there was a most appalling stench. The doctor sniffed and said he thought it was something dead. We examined the cows that were lying down, but they were all alive. Then the doctor made an orderly rake over all the straw. He said that the Germans had a habit of hiding dead men under straw, if they were vacating a place, just by way of providing a pleasant surprise for any tired British soldiers who might make the straw their bed. However, there were no corpses in the cowshed, and we never discovered the cause of the smell, though it was strong and nasty enough to prevent my ever forgetting it.

On coming out of the farm I found the Dorchester Regiment passing by. After lying about in a trench, hardly seeing more than the men in one's own platoon, it was quite a change to see another regiment and have a talk to the officers about their experiences in the past few days. It was interesting to hear how the next-door regiment had fared in the night attack, and if they had met much opposition in gaining the village they had been told to take. One subaltern, with a scrubby ten days' growth of beard on his chin, grinned as though he thought he knew me as he went by, and said : " Who'd have thought we were being brought up to do this ? "

I looked at him, and suddenly recognized a fellow who had been a cadet with me at Sandhurst. It did, indeed, seem droll to look back on the days when we had drilled in the same squad together and studied tactics in the same class, without ever, I am afraid, any

PUSHING FORWARD 151

serious thoughts of war. Well, anyway, now our learning was being put to the test, and as I watched the boy now become a man march by with his company, all muddy from the trenches, with his few worldly possessions slung from his belt, I thought that he, at any rate, was a good advertisement for Sandhurst.

" Where are you going—do you know ? " I called.

He shrugged his shoulders and pointed away across the fields. It was growing dusk, and I began to wonder where we were going. We had been halted by the farm some time now. I turned back to my platoon, who were lying on some straw against a wall. I thought I would go and find some of the other platoon commanders and hear if there was any news. But this plan was frustrated, Evans and the others were nowhere to be found. I asked my sergeant if he knew where the rest of the company was. He said he did not. It was my business, of course, not his, to know, and he—wretched man—having been asleep, knew this perfectly well. After a search round the farm I came to the conclusion that the company had gone off somewhere and that I was left. Here was a pretty kettle of fish. Goyle would not thank me for losing a whole platoon. The company must be found again at once. The difficulty was they might have gone off in any direction. I questioned the men. Some thought they had seen the captain going back the way we had come; others had seen nothing. To go back the way we had come would probably be putting oneself too far back if wanted. I eventually decided to cut straight across a field and reach a road which would take me to the same village as the Dorchesters were going to. In this way I should have them between myself and the enemy, and so eliminate the risk of being cut off, and also should be moving along towards the enemy in the same direction as presumably my company was moving.

It was by now quite dark, and, crossing the field, we nearly fell into an empty trench which the Germans had held. The most noticeable thing about the trench was the murderous field of fire it afforded. The trench had evidently been sighted by a past master in the art of war.

On reaching the road I decided to stay there

PUSHING FORWARD 153

for a while until some one came along from whom I could ask questions. It was rather jumpy work to be isolated by oneself with a platoon without quite knowing where one was. To my great relief, after a few minutes a company from my regiment came along, followed by Goyle at the head of my own company, and I was able to join up. It appeared that in the interval since we had parted the company had been ordered to entrench themselves in three different places, and then moved on again, and so, as Goyle did not seem to mind once I had joined up again safely, I was very glad I had missed all the unnecessary excitement. It was characteristic of Goyle that he never found fault with anything his subalterns did unless it led to trouble. As I had got there all right somehow, and not been wanted in the meantime, he did not blame me for getting lost.

We marched along for a little way down the road, and then swung to the right down another road, which led through a straggling village. The cottages were all in darkness, but they looked very inviting, and I think each man wished heartily that he was going to sleep in one instead of marching on into the night.

After passing through the village we came out on to a straight road flanked by two deep ditches. After going a few hundred yards along this road we were told to halt, climb over the ditch, and entrench. This we did.

When all was snug and compact for the night Goyle and I went back to the village to let the Dorchesters know what we had done. We found several of the officers in the kitchen of a small wine shop. They had got a fire going, and were making coffee, and this, with a bottle of rum found in the cellar, and the remains of the day's rations, promised an excellent supper. I had some bread and cheese left in my haversack, and shared this with Goyle; we were given a mug of coffee each, and joined the others at the table. After the excitements of the evening the coffee and rum were welcome. As we were having supper I heard some groans, and suddenly noticed a huge Uhlan lying flat on his back in the corner. He was breathing with difficulty, and every now and then seemed to be trying to wriggle along the floor. One of the Dorchester officers told me that the man had been found in a ditch and brought in by our men. He was shot straight through the stomach. They had sent up for the doctor, but the latter was unable to come down that night. Supper proceeded smoothly, uninterrupted by the groans of the Uhlan, who was only half-conscious, but at times evidently in great pain.

"I say," said one of the Dorchesters' officers, "I propose sleeping here. I don't much fancy having that fellow in the room all night."

It was then decided to move the Uhlan to an empty house opposite, where he died by himself, and was found on his knees, with his head contorted between them in a last effort to rise, in the morning.

XIV. IN FRONT OF LA BASSEE

AT daybreak the order came to advance. A and C Companies were to form the firing-line, B and D Companies were to be in support. We formed the right of the brigade, and had to get in touch with the Westshires, who were on the left of the —th Brigade, on our right. The initiative of the attack rested with A and C Companies ; our task was to follow behind over the ground they had gained and be ready to come up into line with them should they lose many men or find themselves hard pressed. The enemy we knew to be holding a group of houses about 700 yards away. The ground sloped gently back from these houses to the outskirts of the town. My company, B Company, under Goyle, had been extended during the night, in a field to the right of the road, and had thrown up a low earthwork parapet. We now lay behind this while A and C Companies pushed through us to the front. The parapet proved none too high, for as soon as the men in front showed themselves a brisk fire came from the enemy in the houses. We all lay flat on the ground, and the bullets came phzz-phzz over us, missing us, as it seemed, by an inch or two. There is an old military adage that the man who thinks each bullet he hears is going to hit him is making active service a torture to himself. Now, it is all very well to preach the value of being philosophical in warfare and to recommend the man under fire not to think about being hit, but that peculiar sharp little whistle which a bullet makes as it passes one's ear takes a good deal of getting used to, and one's first instinct as one hears it is to slide as deep and far into the ground as possible. We all lay there with our noses flat in the earth, wondering how the fellows in front were getting on and when it would be our turn to get up. The opportunity came pretty soon, for, as the company in front seemed to be held up by the enemy in the houses, Goyle decided to send round a flanking party, and sent off No. 7 and 8 platoons to work their way round on the right. This plan proved successful, and A Company was able to get ahead. Goyle now signalled for the two platoons, which had remained with him, to advance. We rose and moved forward in extended order for 300 yards and then lay down again.

After a few minutes Goyle exclaimed :

" Hullo!—our fellows have reached the houses." Looking through my glasses, I saw some of our men in the gardens of the houses, and as there was no fighting going on the Germans had evidently withdrawn. Goyle decided that we would push on, and told Evans and me to join up by the houses with two platoons which had gone round by the flank. We were to search the houses thoroughly, and take up a line on the other side of them. On our way forward we came on the results of some work we had heard going on during the night. Just before we reached the houses we found three men from the Westshires in a ditch. One was dead, the others too badly hit to crawl. It appears they had been sent out on patrol the night before, and, coming on the German lines, had got shot down. As I had been out on patrol myself on the other side of the road the same night, I reflected that my patrol had been lucky to escape the same fate.

IN FRONT OF LA BASSEE

The two wounded men had been lying there for some time, and were very glad to be found. The worst side of patrol work is the risk of not being found or it not being possible to bring wounded men in. We sent the two wounded men back to the ambulance, and asked for a party to be sent up to bury the other. I took the dead man's rifle myself. It was very bloody and nasty, but I felt it would be a good companion, as apart from a rifle and bayonet being twice as useful as a revolver and sword (no one carries the latter), a rifle is also a very good disguise for an officer. If he is holding his rifle, as the men always do, at the trail in an advance, he is indistinguishable to the enemy. Especially was this the case at one time, when the enemy had got used to looking out for a gentleman with a revolver in one hand, a walking-stick in the other, and a pair of field-glasses slung round his neck, advancing slightly ahead of the line of men, and waving instructions to them with the stick. Nowadays the wise officer keeps well in a line with his men, and gives as few indications by hand signals to halt or advance, etc., as possible.

I got most of the blood off the rifle with some grass, and, armed with it and the bayonet, I felt much more secure as we made our way through the houses. The Germans had evidently spent a day or two round the houses, for just behind we found a straw-lined ditch, which they had slept in and partially converted to a trench. We lined this ditch, which gave good cover against stray bullets, and waited for further orders. While we were waiting, Edwards, who had charge of the flanking party, pushed out to the right to get in touch with the Westshires, and Evans and I went back to have a look at the houses and see if the enemy had left any souvenirs behind. One of the buildings was the village wine shop, and a party of German officers had evidently used it as their headquarters for the night. They appeared to have had a rare time in the place. Half-emptied glasses of wine had been left on the bar counter and on the table ; bottles and glasses lay smashed on the floor ; every bottle from the shelves behind the bar had been taken down and either drunk or broken and the contents spilt over the floor. Two chairs lay broken, and all the pictures were

IN FRONT OF LA BASSEE 161

smashed, presumably by cockshies with bottles and glasses. From the look of things the officers must have all been extremely drunk.

While we were in the wine shop the order came for us to close up on A Company, who had pushed some distance forward. The ground at this point sloped up to some more cottages and farm buildings which lay at the top of the rise. A and C Companies had worked their way through the cottages and lined out beyond them facing the outskirts of the town. They were unable to go any farther, as the ground in front was a dead flat stretch of root crops, which the Germans could sweep with rifle and machine-gun fire. The cottages in front to a certain extent covered the advance up to this point, but not completely, as Mulligan, in charge of the right platoon of the next supporting company, discovered to his cost. We were advancing in extended order up the rise, my company being well protected by the cottages, but Mulligan had a gap in the buildings in front of him. About half-way across the field he evidently came into range of a German machine-gun. The gun opened a brisk fire, and in as many seconds twenty of his men were down, Mulligan himself getting a bullet through the shoulder, and his servant, who was beside him, being killed. From an infantryman's point of view a Maxim is like water to a mad dog. It will stop him when nothing else will. There is something particularly deterring about the sound of a Maxim, with its ping-ping-ping-ping as it sweeps down a line of advancing troops, spurting lead like a hose-pipe. The great art from an infantryman's point of view is to locate these guns, and avoid going over ground they cover. It is, humanly speaking, hopeless to try to advance straight against them. Word soon goes along a line, " They've got a Maxim along that road," or " Machine-guns are on that corner of the field or gap in the hedge," and the road, or corner of the field, or gap in the hedge is avoided like a plague spot accordingly.

After we had lain behind the cottages on the rise for a little while, the commander of A Company sent back to say he would like a platoon from the supports sent up to him. Goyle told me to take up No. 6. Hutson, who was commanding A Company, was a capital

IN FRONT OF LA BASSEE 163

fellow to work under, and was moving about behind his trenches giving directions to the men as coolly as if he had been on manœuvres instead of only separated by a root field from the first line of the German army. He showed me the bit of trench he wanted my platoon to occupy, gave some instructions about putting out an advanced post, and said the officers of A Company were having a stew cooked in the kitchen of one of the cottages, if I would care to come in when it was dark and all was straight for the night. He said he did not think we should try to advance any farther that night, but hold on where we were.

I lined my men out along the section of trench I was to occupy, which had mostly still to be made, and got them to work. It was growing dusk, and buildings along the outskirts of the town were standing out clearly against the sky-line. Just in front of us was what appeared to be a large factory. As I watched I saw a shell crash against the roof of the factory, followed by another and another. Soon flames sprang from a corner of the building, but still the shells were sent against it, and in ten minutes the whole building was ablaze.

Our guns stopped firing when the smoke and fire showed they had done their work. Dark figures could be seen running about from point to point silhouetted against the flames. Our men fired at the figures, and made jokes about the discomfiture of the enemy, who could not move now without being shown up by the flames, while they themselves were secure in the darkness.

Then as I watched I saw a very dashing piece of work on the part of the enemy, for up galloped a section of horse artillery right into the firing-line, unlimbered, and opened fire. Their target was soon plain : a row of haystacks just behind our lines. In five minutes these stacks, too, were blazing merrily, and our lines were lit up as clearly as the Germans'.

The whole scene made a wonderful stage battle effect, with the two rival lines of trenches and the flames behind each shooting luridly to the sky.

Later Hutson came up to me.

" By Jove ! " he said, " my young subaltern did a good bit of work just now. You know

IN FRONT OF LA BASSEE

when those German guns started on our stacks. Well, he got three men with buckets, filled 'em at a pump, and dashed at the first stack and tried to put it out. A bit of a fireman, to get to work like that while the object he was trying to extinguish was still under shell fire."

I am glad to say that the deed of the young subaltern referred to was mentioned in dispatches and that he received the D.S.O. and the three men with him the D.C.M.

XV. A NIGHT PATROL

THE regiment was acting as advance guard to the brigade, so considerable responsibility rested on Goyle, who was senior officer of the three companies employed. Goyle had been through the war from the beginning, and had learnt the difference between reckless dash and careful handling of men. Goyle had had four of his subalterns killed and most of his original company replaced by reinforcements. He had held the canal bank at Mons and fought slowly backwards from house to house at Le Cateau. What he did not know of the Germans and their methods of fighting no general knew, nor staff officer with red-banded, brass-rimmed cap. Perhaps the generals and their staff officers knew as much theoretically and had learnt a good deal from the result of actions in which the divisions and units under their command had been engaged, but none knew more than Goyle, who was a plain regimental officer and lived daily in the firing-line. Had

A NIGHT PATROL 167

many but he been in command that night the advance guard would have been cut up.

We had covered the first part of our march uneventfully, and were now moving along a stretch of open road which ran between two deep ditches with ploughland on either side. The Dorchesters were following us, and they, we knew, had reached a village about half a mile behind. Goyle was from the first extremely anxious not to let the gap between ourselves and the Dorchesters get too wide. Our orders were to halt on a cross-road at some point farther down along the road on which we were marching. It was quite dark, and we were proceeding very slowly, as we were uncertain of the whereabouts or strength of the enemy. Goyle had got all the men off the road, and was making them move single file by companies along the ditches. We proceeded some distance in this way, but no crossroads could be found, and after a bit Goyle halted and sent back for further instructions. He discovered at the same time that communication had not been maintained with the brigade on the right, and that the Dorchesters showed no inclination to leave the village they had reached, but were disposed to billet there. In fact, everything pointed to a slight muddle having arisen, as a result of which the three companies of my regiment might be severe sufferers in their isolated position if the enemy suddenly attacked. It was the sort of occasion when many officers less experienced than Goyle might have done something which would have led to a disaster. Many, for instance, would have pushed boldly on until they found the cross-roads or met the enemy. They would have said that those were their orders and that it was not for them to wonder whether there was any mistake. However, Goyle was not of this sort. He believed in using his own judgment and acting as circumstances seemed to dictate. His first concern was for the lives of his men, which he would throw away as lightly as his own if necessary, but which he always guarded jealously against the possible perils of tactical mistakes.

" I don't like this," he said once or twice, as we were standing there waiting for the reply to the message he had sent back. " It is all very well, you know, but if they came for us now in any strength we should get scuppered."

A NIGHT PATROL 169

It was dark, and we seemed a long way out along the road from the other troops. I understood what he meant, and saw the danger. Presently the orderly returned with a written message from the Commanding Officer : " You are to go on as far as the R in ——, and remain in the village for the night." Goyle pulled out his map, and we bent over it. —— was a village of a few cottages, apparently about a quarter of a mile down the road. I could see Goyle did not like the order. " It is all very well," he said ; " probably the enemy are in the village—a nice trap we shall be walking into. I shall send on a patrol, and if the village is held I shan't move on till daylight, when we have got some reinforcements up."

It was then decided that I should take out a patrol and go and scout the village. " Take a lance-corporal and a man with you," said Goyle ; " and when you get to the village one of you go into the first house, leaving the other two outside ; if the one who goes into the house does not come out, another is to follow him in, and if he stays too, the third is to come back and tell me. If we hear shots and none of you return we shall know the village is occupied."

"Very good, sir," I said; and, wishing I was anywhere else, I went off to get the patrol. I called my platoon together, explained the work on hand, and asked for volunteers. I got a N.C.O. without difficulty, but there was no response when I asked for a man. Much disgusted at the want of spirit in the men, I was preparing to go off alone with the lance-corporal rather than force anyone to go with me, when a man stepped out of the ranks and made the party complete. Afterwards Jenkins, my soldier servant, from whom I used to get tips about handling the men and various bits of barrack-room gossip, explained to me why I had got an N.C.O. easily enough, but had had difficulty in getting a man. It appeared that the men had a rooted dislike to patrols composed of an officer, a non-commissioned officer, and a man, as they considered the man was always made the victim of the enterprise, being sent on when the danger point was reached to draw fire. He said that had I asked for two men they would have come forward willingly, but, having got the

A NIGHT PATROL 171

N.C.O., no one cared to offer himself to take the place of the private.

I saw what Jenkins meant, and decided to remember the point for future guidance. As a matter of fact, I had decided that we should all go together, anyway until the occasion came for entering the houses, when it would be time enough to arrange who should go first.

Having got my N.C.O. and man together, I explained to them the work that was on foot, and said that at the first shot from the enemy each was to run for himself, and that no one was to wait to reply to the fire; all we had to do was to find out whether or not the place was occupied. Liking the job less each minute, we started off down the road. After going a little way it occurred to me that an old military rule was to keep a Maxim on a road at night, and that we should get rather in the way of this if the enemy had one and opened fire. Accordingly I ordered the patrol off the road on to the ploughland beside. This was a good manœuvre, as we were able to creep over the soft soil noiselessly. We felt our way on for some distance, until I saw two dark objects. These were the first of the houses we had to explore. Praying fervently that they might be empty, I led the way towards them. Suddenly there was a sharp burst of fire ahead along a front of about fifty yards. The shots could not have been fired from more than ten yards range. We had evidently all but walked into a German trench. The enemy had heard us, and blazed into the night. The effect of the shots suddenly fired out of nothing was most startling. As one man we all three turned and bolted in the opposite direction. The corporal dropped his rifle, I lost my cap; the private, being a fine sprinter, got slightly ahead, and we all three ran like mad. After a couple of hundred yards I went head over heels into a ditch. The corporal paused a moment to see if I had been hit, but continued as soon as I got up; the man kept an unchecked course for home, looking neither to the right nor the left. In the fall I slightly dislocated my knee, but this was as nothing, and, hardly hindered by a limp, I followed at full speed in the wake of the rout, the man now holding a good lead, the corporal lying second, and myself a bad third. I bethought me as I ran that we should probably draw the fire of our

A NIGHT PATROL 173

own men, who would think we were the enemy, and halloaed : " Goyle—Goyle—this is the patrol returning."

" Shut up, you blithering idiot," I heard his voice from the road ; " do you want all Germany to know where we are ? "

I flung myself on the ground beside him and breathlessly reported what had happened. " H'm," said Goyle, " just what I thought. I shan't try to occupy that village to-night."

Just then the Major commanding the regiment and Adjutant, who had been back with the reserve company, came up. " Well, what is it, Goyle ? " said the Major testily ; " why don't you push on into the village ? "

The Major was a very gallant officer, with considerable war experience behind him. To his mind " dash " was the great thing. But the Major's experiences had been chiefly in savage warfare, and he had no knowledge of German methods. He had only come out from England two days before to take the place of our Colonel, who had been wounded.

Goyle pointed to me, said that he had sent out a patrol, and that the village was occupied. " Oh," said the Adjutant, " probably only two or three half-scared Uhlans. You ought to have tackled them and brought back their helmets "—this to me.

I offered with acid politeness to indicate the position of the " Uhlans " so that the Adjutant could go out himself and get their helmets.

" I think the enemy are entrenched, sir," said Goyle to the Major.

" Well, have at them and drive them out," the latter answered.

" We are rather isolated here, sir, and we are too weak to attack the village by ourselves."

" Maybe — maybe — I should push on, though," the Major answered.

" If you will excuse me, sir, I feel the responsibility rather too great—if you would take command of the attack, sir." This was a master-stroke on Goyle's part, as it brought home to the Major the responsibility of throwing his men without proper support against a position of unknown strength in the dark. He hummed and hawed, and finally decided to leave things as they were till daylight, and returned with the Adjutant to the reserve company.

A NIGHT PATROL 175

As things turned out, it was lucky for all of us that Goyle had been firm about advancing farther; for, so far from there only being a few half-scared Uhlans ahead of us, we discovered afterwards that the Germans were in force and strongly entrenched, and any attempt at attack by the three companies must have failed disastrously.

When the Major had gone Goyle decided to move back, so as to get in closer touch with the Dorchesters. We withdrew, therefore, to the outskirts of the village, lined out on the ploughland on either side of the road, and set the men to entrench.

XVI. WITH THE SUPPORTS

THE Support trenches lay along a road about fifty yards behind the firing-line. The trenches themselves were made partly from a ditch by the side of the road, and partly excavated from a ploughed field which ran out in the direction of the enemy. The firing-line trenches were beyond in the ploughed field itself; beyond the ploughland again came a stretch of root crop, and at the end of this the enemy.

The Westshires were holding the firing-line, and we were close up behind them in support. In spite of the narrow margin between the supports and firing-line life was a good deal easier for the supports. Indeed, we felt ourselves onlookers compared to the Westshires in front. The ground sloped gently down from their trenches to the road. They could not move without showing up against the sky-line, while we, by crouching, could move about our trenches with comparative freedom.

But the chief blessing of being in support

WITH THE SUPPORTS 177

lay in the fact that we were not directly responsible for giving the first alarm. The onus of waiting and watching for the German attack lay on the Westshires, and our men felt themselves to be more or less onlookers for the day, and lay about reading the newspapers and smoking. Evans and I found plenty to occupy ourselves during the afternoon. There was a small farm just by the side of our trench, protected from view by a row of cottages. The owners of the farm had gone the day before, when there had been an attack on the village, and left their home just as it was. We took over the farm for our own use, got a fire going in the kitchen, and set our servants to work to prepare dinner. Jenkins, my servant, had been a chauffeur valet before the war, and had great ideas how things ought to be done. These ideas had on occasion been reduced to making tea during a halt by the roadside in a small black and dirty pot, which he kept fastened to his pack, but with a kitchen stove to cook over and an unlimited supply of crockery he was in his element.

Having annexed the farm as an officers' mess and installed Jenkins in the kitchen we made a tour of the yard. Here we found several things which wanted doing. First there was the farm dog, who had been left behind chained to his kennel. The dog had had nothing to eat for two days, and was ravenous. We got him a large bone and loosed him, so that if we had to scurry he would not have to stay behind. Then we found some cows in a shed in great pain from want of milking. There was a man in my platoon who had been a dairyman, and I set him to work on them. In a barn we found a quantity of straw, which we sent down to the trenches. Finally we got soap and towels from a bedroom, and repaired to the pump for a much-needed cleaning.

After washing ourselves we went out for a stroll before dinner. We found a little group standing in the lee of the cottage across the road—the Adjutant of the Westshires, the regimental doctor, two stretcher-bearers, and an N.C.O. A man had been hit in the trench just ahead of us, and the doctor had been sent for to come up from the field-ambulance. The doctor had just sent word up to the trench to find out the nature of the man's injuries. If he was severely wounded and required imme-

WITH THE SUPPORTS 179

diate attention, the doctor was prepared to send up his stretcher-bearers to have him brought down, but it would be a difficult job and exposing men's lives, and the doctor wanted, if possible, to leave the man there till dark. Doctors attached to regiments have many difficult points to settle, and occasions like this often arise when it is hard for them to decide whether to risk more lives to save one. They are called upon sometimes to go up and attend to cases in all sorts of impossible places, and in the firing-line the old cry of "Send for the doctor" is not quite so easily answered as in other places.

We left the group by the cottage waiting for the reply about the nature of the wounded man's injuries. Not a head showed from the trench where he was lying. The trench itself, though only twenty yards or so away, was hardly visible in the field. Glad it was not our turn to lie like logs in it all the day, we went on down the village street. Nearly all the cottages were empty, but in one we came on a group of inhabitants who had remained. They had all collected in a kitchen and were having a last meal round their table. They had got a little bread and some coffee, which they were sharing with three private soldiers, who in exchange had contributed a tin of bully beef. It made a strange sight to see the weeping, frightened women and the tired dusty soldiers who had come to defend them. The women had given the men a place round the fire, and were waiting on them attentively. The privates could speak no French and the peasants no English, so conversation was impossible, but an interchange of thought could be read in the eyes of both parties ; the women looking on the men sadly and devoutedly, realizing they had come there perhaps to give their lives for them, and across the men's faces would come a look of appreciation for the hot comforting coffee, and at other times a look of inscrutable purposefulness, which is hard to describe, but which all our men wear in France, and which is symbolic of the spirit which is carrying them through the campaign.

Seeing officers outside, one of the women came out. I said " good-morning " to her in French, and with a delighted "*Ah, Monsieur, vous parlez Français,*" she addressed herself to me excitedly. It appeared that her husband

WITH THE SUPPORTS 181

had been missing since the day before. She was very anxious about him. Two officers had come to the cottage, asked him some questions, and then taken him away with them. She had not seen the man since. What did I think could have become of him? I asked her some questions about the officers who had taken her husband away, and from her description gathered that they were a captain and subaltern in the British Army. As the Westshire Regiment was the only regiment that I knew had been in the village since the Germans left it, I felt sure the officers the woman referred to must be from that regiment. Accordingly I went back to ask the adjutant of the Westshires if he could give any information on the subject. He told me that when the regiment had got up to the village the day before they had searched the cottages and found a man in one of the upper rooms behaving suspiciously with a lamp by a window which looked on the German lines. They had taken the man off with them and sent him back to the rear, where he would probably be tried for his life for a spy. This put me in an awkward position, as I did not know what to tell the poor woman, who, whatever her husband had done, was herself innocent of any evil intentions. I contended myself with telling her that her husband was in British hands, and that she might rest assured he would be fairly treated.

Another difficulty then presented itself. The little party of women in the cottage all wished to leave the village. They had collected their few most cherished possessions together in a cart and proposed to go off as soon as it was dark. But this could not be permitted, as the noise of the cart, which would have to go along a road that ran through our lines, would have attracted the enemy's attention and drawn their fire on our men. The women refused to leave the cart with their treasures behind and the situation seemed to have reached an *impasse*. Finally, after interviewing the colonel of the Westshires, I was able to get permission for them to take their cart, provided they kept it along the grassy side of the road.

I shall never forget the little procession as it moved off after dark. First the cart, drawn by an old horse with a woman leading it followed by a sorrowful little procession of women and children with quick, frightened

WITH THE SUPPORTS

steps and bowed heads. They were leaving their village, their homes, nearly all their belongings, and the little plots of garden and weaving looms which were their livelihood, to go out to the country beyond—which had always appeared in the little hemisphere of their lives as a strange land dealing hardly with wandering strangers. They were going away and would, perhaps, never see their village again. (Alas, indeed, they never did.) Well may they have wondered what they had done to bring such misery about their heads—misery embodied in the Scriptural curse of old : War, rape, desolation, and famine.

However, there is little sentiment in war, and as we watched them go we had not more than a passing thought for them. We were chiefly conscious of having a farm to ourselves, and the prospect of a night of unusual comfort for the firing-line.

Jenkins had made great preparations while we were away, and had a two-course dinner ready for us—roast chickens and stewed apples. We fell to on this heartily, and then sat round the kitchen stove drinking hot rum and water. We turned in early, two of us using two beds and the other two mattresses on the floor. With the Westshires in front of us we were care-free for the night. An hour before dawn we were called, and went back to the trenches to rouse the men to stand to arms. Then we went to bed again and slept till eight.

We pulled the kitchen table out to the garden for breakfast, and made a capital meal of fried eggs and bread and marmalade. We sat over breakfast smoking cigarettes and drinking last cups of tea. It seemed odd to be living such a leisurely life 700 yards from the enemy, but the cottages in front secured us as long as they did not use artillery. However, this was to come later. An artillery observing officer came to fix up a field telephone just by our breakfast table. He expressed his opinion that the enemy had got their guns up, and that the day would be lively.

" Well," said Goyle, " perhaps we had better get back to the trench for a bit anyway." Our trench was only ten yards off, just the other side of the garden, and we stepped into it. Scarcely had we done so than—crash !—a black Maria fell fair and square on the farm where we had been sleeping. It was a matter of seconds, and

WITH THE SUPPORTS 185

what happened to the artillery observing officer, whom we had left behind adjusting his telephone, I do not know. Perhaps he lived. Artillery observing officers have a knack of living in places where any other man would be killed. However, we had no time to speculate on his fate, for a minute later another high-explosive shell burst fifty yards over the trench, followed by a second twenty-five yards over us. The enemy were shortening their range. The men stirred uneasily in their dug-outs. No rat in a trap could feel worse than an infantryman in a trench when a big gun is searching for him with high explosive. B A N G ! A shell burst on the other side of the road—ten yards from us. The next would undoubtedly do it.

"Here," I called to Goyle, "what about this ? They are getting our range."

"We had better quit," he said. "Don't let the men run—file out slowly to the right, and lie down behind that bank there. The other platoon must stay ; they are not being molested at present."

With as much dignity as possible, considering I expected a black Maria in the back at any moment, I led the men out of the trench, and we threaded our way gingerly back to the bank indicated, from which we watched the vicious demolition of our empty trench.

XVII. BETWEEN ACTIONS

JUST before dusk I was sent up with my platoon to join D Company, who had more line than the number of men in the company could safely hold. After being shown the section of ground where my men were wanted, I went off to join the other officers of the company, who were having a bit of dinner in a cottage, leaving the men to improve the trench, and telling Jenkins, my soldier-servant, to make a good big dug-out for us both.

It is interesting now to record that the officer commanding the company to which I was lent was a man I had known in times of peace and loathed to the point which drives a man to homicide. He was a fine great fellow, but a bit rough with subalterns, and had, as he no doubt thought for my own good, made my life a burden to me when I joined the regiment. I often used to say to myself, when discipline and mess etiquette prevented my replying to his remarks to me in the ante-

room in days of peace : " My sainted aunt—
if ever I get alone with you in the desert, my
friend, I'll shoot." For two or three years
we never spoke to each other, and then
suddenly I found myself sent up to serve under
him in the firing-line in front of La Bassée.
How circumstances alter cases. He had me
in his hands then. Had he been the bully I
thought him, there were a hundred dirty jobs
he could have made me do. He could have
sent me out on patrol or with messages to the
next regiment. There were many nasty things
which had to be done that night. But all he
said, when I came up and reported myself as
having been sent up to reinforce him with a
platoon, was : " Hullo, old chap. Look here,
I just want you to put your men along here,
do you see ? "—indicating the gap he wanted
filled—" and when you've done that, come into
the cottage and have a bit of dinner."

It was hospitable at a time when each man
carried his own rations for the day, and I had
none left. The putting out of patrols and
walking up and down the line he did himself
rather than ask me, whose job it was ,as his
subaltern for the time being. A few days

BETWEEN ACTIONS 189

later, when I was hit, he was one of the first people to come up to me, and he was himself killed five minutes later, gallantly leading a charge to drive the Germans back from the spot where the wounded were dying.

While we were having dinner, the other subalterns and myself compared notes about the different quarters we had for the night ; one saying he had not room to lie down in his dug-out ; another that he had found a lot of hay and made a fine lair ; and the machine-gun officer saying that he was best off of all, as he had his guns peeping from the window of a bedroom above, and proposed to spend the night in bed by the side of them.

When the meal was over and we had had a smoke, we dispersed to the different sections of the defence we were holding. I found that Jenkins had made a beautiful dug-out, lined it with straw, and roofed it with some V-shaped pieces of thatch which the peasants in that part of France use to protect their fruit. He had allowed just the right space for me to lie down, and done everything he could think of that would enable us to spend the night comfortably. Jenkins in private life was a chauffeur-valet, of a fastidious, easily ruffled, and slightly grasping disposition. However, though he would have died rather than wear some of my old clothes, he was so well able to adapt himself to the war that he won the D.C.M.

Having looked along the trench and moved the group sentry to a point just near the dug-out, I settled down beside Jenkins on the straw. Jenkins and I shared a little rum I had left over in my flask from the day's rations, and, feeling very warm and good inside, closed our eyes. My guardian angel was with me that evening, for I could not sleep, and Jenkins, who could, kept grunting, which got on my nerves so near my ear, so I decided to take some of the straw and lie down behind the trench outside.

It was very dark, and the outline of the group sentry could just be seen against the parapet. From where I had been in the dug-out I could not see either of the sentries. As we were in the front line, with nothing but a stretch of ploughland between ourselves and the Germans and all the men in the trench were asleep, those two sentries were pretty

BETWEEN ACTIONS 191

important. I lay there watching them with half-closed eyes. One was resting with his head on the parapet (which is permissible as long as the other keeps a sharp watch), but to my horror I saw the other, after about ten minutes, turn round, sit against the parapet with his back to the enemy, and deliberately drop his head on his arms and go to sleep. We now had no one keeping watch over us at all, and there was nothing to stop the Germans creeping over and bayoneting a trench full of sleeping men. My first instinct was to march the sentry straight off under arrest, then I remembered the penalty, and that he was only a boy, and that it was many days and nights since the men had had proper sleep. So I crept towards him, gave him a crack under the jaw with my fist, which would effectively keep him awake for the rest of his turn of duty, said, " You dare to turn round with your back to the enemy," and lay down again. I remember waking up uneasily every quarter of an hour through the night and looking to see if the sentry was keeping awake, and being reassured by a plaintive snuffling as the boy looked ahead and rubbed his chin.

At 4 A.M. a regiment came to take over our lines, and we were sent back in reserve. We marched back about a mile to a big empty farm, where we were told we were going to spend the day. I had rejoined my own company, and, as caterer for the company officers' mess, set about getting breakfast for the five officers.

One of the latter, Edwards, was fresh out to the Front, and had not quite got out of the way of being waited on by mess waiters. We had sat down to the meal, which I had got ready on a table in the garden. Edwards came up late, and found there was no tea left, so I sent him to the kitchen to get some. Later we all wanted another cup, and I dispatched him again, as he was the junior of the party, and I did not see why I should do all the work. He came back and said there was no one there; what was he to do about the tea? I said, "Make it." He said he did not know how to. I took him gently by the arm and led him to the kitchen to show him. When we had finished breakfast, Goyle and the senior platoon commanders lit their pipes, while I cleared away the things. Edwards pulled out

BETWEEN ACTIONS 193

his pipe too. But I said, " No, my boy ; you help here." I had an armful of crockery as I spoke, which I was taking to wash up. Looking rather hurt, he followed me into the kitchen, carrying a teaspoon. " I don't see why I should do all this," he said, as we were washing up. " Don't you, my boy ? " I said, sharply. " And do you see any reason for me doing it ? " He did not answer. " It may not be one of the things you learnt at Sandhurst," I continued, " but when you've been engaged in this campaign a little longer, you'll discover that if you don't bally well shift for yourself you'll starve."

He was a good boy all the same, and got a bullet through the knee leading his men at ——, and is a guest of the Kaiser now.

For lunch we had a Mc'Conochie. Mc'-Conochie is a form of tinned stew, and very succulent if properly cooked, as vegetables and a rich gravy are contained in the tin. The usual way is to put the tin in a saucepan of boiling water, let it boil for a while, and then take it out and open it. However, that day as we were in a hurry—we had had orders to take over the Westshires' trenches at midnight

—I put the tin straight on the fire, thinking to warm it up quicker. We were sitting round talking when Evans suddenly exclaimed, "Gad, look at that tin!"

We looked and saw it swelling itself out. The gravy had turned to steam, and the thing was on the point of bursting. I seized the tongs and snatched it from the fire, placing it on the table. The thing still seemed to be swelling gently.

"Quick," said Goyle, "prick it—it will go off."

I opened my clasp knife and gave it a jab. There was a sound like an engine-whistle, and a jet of gravy steam shot into Goyle's eye.

"Oh, oh, you blithering idiot," he shouted, dancing about the room with his hand clapped to his eye.

I watched the tin, wondering if all the stew had turned to steam. However, happily it had not, and we had a good meal.

After lunch I strolled across to have a look at the field-dressing station, which was in one of the farm outbuildings.

The doctor was attending to one or two

BETWEEN ACTIONS 195

wounded who came in, but not having a very busy time. I watched him at work for a little while. He was wonderfully thorough considering that his ward consisted of an open yard and his material a box of dressings, a pair of scissors, and a bottle of iodine. He stripped off the field bandages of each man that came in and put on fresh dressings. One fellow walked in with a bullet straight through his chest. He was deathly pale, but he stood up while they took off his jacket and cut his shirt away, and looked down quite unconcerned at the blood pouring from the hole through him.

At four o'clock we were told we were wanted in the firing-line again. Goyle made the men take off their greatcoats and advised the officers to put away their mackintoshes.

This last piece of advice was very sound. An officer wearing a mackintosh is a conspicuous target in a line of men, and many have met their death through doing it. Officers will carry rifles, cover their field-glasses with khaki cloth, wear web equipment, and take all sorts of precautions to make themselves as like the men as possible, and then the first time a shower of rain comes put on their mackintoshes and forget to take them off again when they advance. They might just as well wear surplices.

XVIII. "THE —TH BRIGADE WILL ATTACK ——"

WE thought we should have to attack that day, as we knew the powers that be were most anxious for —— to be taken.

The regiment had been, so to speak, in the forefront of the battle for the past two or three days ; that is to say, we had not had any troops between ourselves and the enemy, and, though the fighting had never been of a brisk nature, nevertheless the men were feeling the strain of constant watchfulness and going without sleep. Even if there is not much firing it is not a restful feeling to have nothing but a stretch of open ploughland between oneself and the enemy, and to feel one may be called upon to advance over the ploughland at any minute. It was a nasty stretch of open country, swept and raked from every corner by the enemy's machine-guns, and to lie there waiting for the order to get up and cross it was rather like sitting inspecting a stiff fence.

Greatly to our relief the Westshire Regiment had been sent up to relieve us at 4 A.M. and we had gone back in support. We had handed over the trenches to them without much reluctance, and with an easy prescience that we had had our share of work, and that it was the turn for a regiment fresh from reserve to come up and take our place.

After being relieved we were marched back to a sugar refinery a mile behind, and here we fully expected to spend the day. The men were issued out rations, and the officers made preparations for breakfast. There was a nice house belonging to the manager of the sugar refinery, and in a kitchen we found some crockery and a fire, also the caretaker of the manager's house and his wife. The latter made us a pot of tea, and with our morning issue of cold bacon, a tin of marmalade, and a loaf of bread there were the materials for a good breakfast for the five of us—Goyle, Evans, myself, and the other two platoon commanders.

Our dream of lolling round the sugar refinery all day in reserve was early dispelled. We had barely finished breakfast when the order came

—TH BRIGADE WILL ATTACK —— 199

that we were to pack up and march off. We went back the way we had come towards the line we had been holding overnight.

As we were marching along the rumour spread that we were going back in support of the Westshires, and that there was an attack impending. We halted in some dead ground, and lined a ditch four or five hundred yards behind the line the Westshires were holding. As we were lying there an orderly came up with a message which Goyle was to read and pass on. Goyle showed me the bit of paper before folding it up again. The message ran : " The —th Brigade will attack —— at 10 A.M. in support of the French attack on —— on their right."

It was then nine o'clock, so we had an hour to wait. Goyle was much excited by the message, and said we were certain to be sent up to swell the Westshires' line. The men were still wearing the greatcoats they had had on during the night, and he ordered them to be taken off and put away in the packs. He also advised the platoon commanders to take off their mackintoshes, which show up an officer clearly.

While these preparations were going on I took a stroll down the ditch to battalion headquarters, hoping to find somewhere to leave my greatcoat instead of having to carry it. Battalion headquarters were behind a small house at the junction of a cross-roads. Here other people had collected—the stout officer, the doctor, and an artillery observing officer. The artillery observing officer was in telephonic communication with a heavy battery about two miles back, to which he was sending back messages about possible targets and the effect of fire. Outside the scout officer was making an early lunch off a piece of ham which he had found in the mess-box. I joined him, contributing a biscuit.

"The Major is an ass, you know," he said ; "he will go showing himself."

He pointed to our senior major, a very gallant officer indeed, but a man who had, as the scout officer said, an unfortunate tendency to expose himself to fire. He was at the moment standing at the cross-roads, beyond the shelter of the cottage, looking through his field-glasses in the direction of the enemy's lines. The cross-roads at which he

—TH BRIGADE WILL ATTACK

was standing was a most exposed place. The Major was a smart, dapper-looking man, and he stood with his legs apart, one hand holding the glasses, the other brushing his moustache. Suddenly there was a sharp ping; he dropped the glasses, raised his right foot sharply, and swore. Then he came limping in.

"Curse the brutes—curse the brutes," he said, sitting on the ground and nursing his foot; "they have shot me through the big toe."

The doctor went to the Major's assistance and the scout officer peered round the corner of the house to see if he could make out where the shot had come from. Presently he came back.

I think they have got a Maxim up in that church tower, sir," he said.

There was a fine church in the town the enemy were holding, and the tower stood high up above the other buildings.

"Have they, by Gad—the brutes," said the Major, still nursing his injured foot, which was causing him acute pain. "Here, let me look" he limped to the corner. A Maxim could plainly be heard firing from somewhere in front, ping-ping-ping—ping-ping-ping.

"By Jove, I believe you are right," said the Major. "Here, just send that gunnery officer to me."

The artillery observing subaltern came up.

"Look here, they've got a Maxim in that church tower—see, over there—thing hit me in the foot just now. Can you telephone back and get your guns to it?"

"Yes, sir," said the gunnery subaltern.

Soon four heavy guns were playing on the church tower, and the tower crumbled. So are churches and other things destroyed in war time.

It was now nearly ten, and we returned to our trench. Soon bullets came whistling overhead, and we knew the attack had been launched. We lay low in the dug-outs waiting till we were wanted. Knowing the ground, I could picture clearly what was going on in front, and I did not envy the Westshires their task. I could imagine them getting out of their trenches and advancing in line over that murderous stretch of ploughland. When we had been in the trenches they were then leaving we had hardly dared show our noses above them; but now the Westshires had the order,

—TH BRIGADE WILL ATTACK —— 203

and out they had to go, and forward. Phzz-phzz-phzz. The bullets began to come over more quickly, and we could hear the answering fire of the Westshires. It may have been half an hour that we lay there, and then a hot, dusty figure crawled round the corner of the trench.

"Is the Captain of B Company there ?"

"Yes, I'm here," Goyle answered.

The new arrival squatted down in the trench. It was the Adjutant of the Westshires. He pulled out his pouch and started to fill his pipe. His hands shook so that he could hardly get the tobacco into the bowl. I shall never forget the way he breathed—hard, noisy gasps. The man was evidently at breaking-point.

"How is it going ?" Goyle asked.

"Oh, it's hell," the Adjutant of the Westshires answered.

"It is impossible to expect men to advance over such ground. We have only got about twenty yards. We have had a hundred down already—Leary and Blake are gone—Jones and Barty wounded. It is no good—they can't carry on. Look here ; what I came back for was, would you send an officer with me, so

that I can show him where we want your men ?
Our fellows are rather shaken. I think it
would be a good thing if they would close up
behind. One never knows what might happen.

I could read the Adjutant's thoughts. He
dreaded lest his men should break. He knew
if they had to advance farther they would
be shot down like rabbits. Poor man, he as
Adjutant of the regiment was responsible for
the men's lives and conduct. The regiment
was in danger of being wiped out. No wonder
his hand shook, and he breathed in great gasps.
Never have I seen a man so cruelly strained.
He grew calmer as he sat there, and presently
Goyle sent me back with him.

The Adjutant of the Westshires was quite
calm as we returned to the firing-line. We
found the Colonel of the regiment sitting on
the ground behind a wall. He held a message
in his hands. "Look there!" He read out
the message to the Adjutant.

"Th —th Brigade will continue their attack
on ——— at 11.30 A.M. The attack will be
pressed home at all costs."

Both men looked at each other. They knew
they had received the regiment's death warrant.

—TH BRIGADE WILL ATTACK —— 205

No attack could succeed over such ground. The Colonel looked at his watch. I looked at the little iron-grey man sitting there waiting for the hour when he was to send his regiment to their doom. Then the Adjutant took me quietly, and showed me the places where he wished our men to come up. He was quite calm now as we peeped round the corner of a house at the lines which had to be taken at all costs. The firing had stopped now. The Westshires were lying out in the ploughland at the point they had reached. The Germans lined their trenches waiting for them to move.

But the time never came. Ten minutes later a staff officer had come up, inspected the ground, and cancelled the second order for the attack.

XIX. BY THE SKIN OF OUR TEETH

WE were moved to the village very suddenly. There was no reason that we could see for the move. However, this transpired later. It was getting dusk when we reached the village. A and C Companies were sent at once up to the firing-line, and B and D Companies were lined along a ditch in support. The ditch had been prepared for habitation by the regiment who had held it before. At one point they had thrown some boards across the ditch and made a house underneath. This proved a very welcome shelter when later it came on to rain. We lay in the ditch for an hour or two listening to the last shells before nightfall, from one of our heavy batteries, singing overhead. The shells were sent in groups of three, and we could plainly hear each, whizz-whizz-whizz, chasing each other through the air, perhaps not more than twenty yards apart. We were comfortable enough where we were, and idly

BY THE SKIN OF OUR TEETH

speculated on what errand of destruction the shells were bent. They sounded nasty great things to have coming in the wrong direction, and we wished the Germans joy of them.

About eight I felt hungry, and got out of the trench to have a look round. I had two tins of Mc'Conochie in my haversack, which I put in a pan of boiling water. Across a field to the front I saw a farm, and decided to go over and explore. In the field there were two or three curious heaps of straw, which proved to be the burial piles of dead cows, killed by shell fire, and covered over by the farmer in this rather ineffective fashion. The cows were getting smelly, and I did not stay long looking at them. I found the farm occupied by two old men and an old woman. One of the old men, over eighty, they told me, had taken to his bed and lain there with the shutters up for three days. He was half-dead from fright, and could not be induced to move. The old woman said they had had Germans billeted in the farm a week before. They had treated her and her old husband none too gently, driving them out of the house while they made soup in her cauldron. She had managed to hide one or two little bits of bread, and was making supper off a crust and some coffee. She put the fire at my disposal for getting supper ready for Goyle and the other officers in the company. They all came across a quarter of an hour later, Evans with a great possession—a tin of cocoa. There was plenty of milk to be had from the farm—indeed, it was a godsend to the old people to get a man to milk their cows—and we soon had a beautiful jug of thick, steaming cocoa. We then prepared the Mc'Conochie, and what proved to be our last meal all together was a good one.

It was getting late when we had finished, and we had to hurry back to the support trench. On the way, as I was going along at a quick trot, I came head over heels over a big object and nearly impaled myself on a spike. Apart from the smell of the cow, it was really most dangerous lying out there at night-time and I sent a party of men back to bury it.

The trenches we were to take over lay just beyond the village along the crest of a slope. The section my company was responsible for ran just in front of three haystacks. A company extended away to our right, and the

BY THE SKIN OF OUR TEETH

Dorchester Regiment continued the line to our left. The officer of the regiment we were relieving said to me : " You see those stacks—well, I should keep clear of them ; the enemy have them set." I nodded, very tired at finding myself back in the firing-line, where we had been almost continuously for ten days, and not particularly interested in what the enemy had set or what they had not. In fact, as soon as I had seen the men distributed along the trench, and had given one or two orders about its improvement, I made straight for the centre stack, pulled as much hay as I could out of the side of it, rolled myself up, and went to sleep.

I was awakened by a sharp blow in the back. Looking up I saw Evans drawing his foot back to give me a second and harder kick.

" Get up, you blithering fool," he said ; " your men are out all over the place."

I jumped to my feet, and, fastening my belt as I ran, dashed for the trench. I owed a lot to Evans for waking me. As Evans said, the men were all walking about outside the trench. I got them in immediately, and was preparing to follow when I thought of my bed, and went off to fetch it. One never knew when the next chance of leaving the trench might come. I was bending down, gathering a good armful of hay, when there was a report, a sensation like red-hot iron running through one, followed by acute pain, and I pitched head-forward into the hay. I had been hit. Very frightened and hurt, I crawled as fast as I could round to the side farthest from the enemy and sat down. I examined my wounds—a bullet through each leg. The shots were low down and did not look very serious. They hurt infernally, and I made a mental note to call the next man who said he never noticed he had been hit in the heat of an action a liar. I examined the wounds. Were they serious enough to warrant a visit to the field-dressing station and a possible return to England ? I hoped devoutly they were. An attempt to stand soon satisfied me, and I fell down again, much relieved. All these thoughts were a matter of seconds; in the meanwhile there was a good deal going on round the stack. An enemy battery was playing round it with high-explosive shrapnel. The shells burst first one side, then the other, in front, behind, in all

BY THE SKIN OF OUR TEETH

directions. The noise was deafening, and the lead in the air was just like a hailstorm; however, it was a stout stack, and kept me dry, though I confess I doubted getting away alive. After a few minutes the firing stopped, and, throwing myself on my side, I rolled as fast as I could for a support trench. I pitched headfirst into the trench and landed on the top of two privates who were sheltering in the bottom expecting more shrapnel over at any minute. They were not expecting me, and thought their last hour had come when I fell on top of them. Getting our breath, we all three cursed each other. Then, seeing I was an officer, they became respectful. I explained I was wounded, and they helped me off with my puttees and bound up the wounds with the first-aid bandage which I ripped from my coat. In the meanwhile word was sent back for stretcher-bearers. As the firing had stopped these came up immediately, lifted me out of the trench, put me on a stretcher, and started off with me. We had to go down a road in full view of the enemy. For some providential reason they never fired at us, though I was about the last wounded man to be brought down that road. Halfway down the road the stretcher-bearers began to show signs of feeling my weight. I coaxed them on a few more yards, but when they came to the lee of a cottage they put me down and shook their heads; another bearer came to the rescue, and with the extra help the party proceeded. A hundred yards more brought us to a cottage which was being used as a field-dressing station. The cottage was beginning to fill, and wounded men lay about all over the floor.

"Oh, Gawd! Oh—! ——ooh!!"

"Shut up, can't yer?" a man shouted from the far corner of the room.

"I've got a 'ole in me big enough to put yer 'and in," the sufferer explained, and began again to groan and swear.

"Got a cigarette, mate?" A man deathly pale on a stretcher held out his hand to a comrade who was slightly wounded and standing beside him. The latter extricated a Woodbine from a crumpled packet and passed it down. The man on the stretcher lit the cigarette and puffed at it phlegmatically. It was doubtful whether he would live, and

BY THE SKIN OF OUR TEETH 213

though he did not know this, he knew he must not have anything to eat or drink for many hours.

About fifteen or twenty of us were lying on the floor of a cottage. Outside, four or five hundred yards up the street, a lively fight was in progress for the possession of the village. After the firing-line the cottage seemed a haven of peace and safety.

" Hullo, they've got you."

" Morning, Doctor."

A young fellow, fresh from his training at a hospital, was standing beside me. He was our regimental doctor, and I'd always thought of him as a lucky fellow who rode on a horse when we were on the march, got his rations regularly at all times, and during a scrap enjoyed the security of the extra few hundred yards which he was supposed to have between his dressing-station and the firing-line. Well, here he was to look after me, anyhow.

" Got a bit of work to do to-day, Doctor," I said as he bound me up.

" Yes," he answered, adjusting a blanket as a pad under me, " there, just keep in that position and the bleeding will soon stop." He turned to the man next me.

"I've got some across the way, too," he said, as the orderly handed him fresh bandages. "They've been shelling the poor beggars, knocking all the slates off the roof."

As he spoke some shrapnel crashed against the roof of our cottage, sending a few tiles rattling to the ground. The doctor looked up.

"I think we're all right here," he said. "We've got a double roof. I always try to pick a cottage with a double roof. But those poor devils over the way are getting awful scared; I think I'll slip across to them."

The bit of road he had to "slip across" was catching most of the shells which the cottage did not, and was also the channel for a steady stream of rifle and machine-gun fire. I began to see there wasn't much in it, whether one was a doctor or a platoon commander.

More especially did I realize a doctor's difficulties when, later in the day, just as our doctor had finished looking at my dressings, a message came that the field-dressing station belonging to the regiment on our left had been set alight by a shell. He hastily or-

BY THE SKIN OF OUR TEETH 215

ganized a party of stretcher-bearers and orderlies and went off at once. Later he came back. He said it had been terrible to see the wounded lying helpless in the barn waiting for the flames, but somehow they had managed to rescue all and move them to a safer place, though the whole operation had to be carried out under rifle and shell fire. Each time a regiment is seriously engaged with the enemy at least 100 men are hit, often four times the number. The regimental doctor is supposed to bind up each one of these, and often when times are slack and a stray man here or there gets hit he will be sent for to come up to the trenches.

" 'Allo, Jock," loud greetings were shouted by every one in the room to a little man standing in the doorway with a bandolier across his chest and rifle with bayonet still fixed. He was a grubby little fellow, with blood and mud caked all down his cheek, ragged clothes, and—as I had seen as he came up the cottage steps—a pronounced limp. It was Private Mutton, scallawag, humorist, and well-known character in the regiment.

" Yus, they got me," he said in answer to

inquiries, " fro' me calf," he pointed to his leg, " and right acrost the top of me 'ead "—he raised his cap and showed where a bullet had parted his hair, grazing the scalp. " But I give the bloke somethink what did it." Private Mutton grinned at his bayonet. " Got 'im fair, right fro' 'is stomick."

I could not help feeling delighted, for I recognized in the muddy, gory, highly-pleased-with-himself little man the original of Thomas Atkins, of whose doings along the Indian frontier I had read thrilling accounts by Mr. Kipling, and whose quaint mannerisms I had often laughed at as represented on the stage of music-halls at home. . . .

At 9 P.M. the ambulances came up.

The doctor went round quickly attending to each man. He bound up my wounds afresh and had me carried into an inner room I lay there all day, and never shall I forget the experience. I could see nothing except a bit of the wall on the opposite side of the street. But I could hear. Just after I had been brought in fresh firing broke out. Rifle fire this time, sharp and insistent. Then there was a sound of stamping feet, and I heard an

BY THE SKIN OF OUR TEETH 217

officer rallying the men at the corner of the street. The firing continued all day and sometimes seemed to rage almost at the door of the cottage. I gathered that the Germans were attacking the village in masses, and that it was touch-and-go whether we could hold out. Sometimes there would be a rush of men outside the window, and I would look to see if the pale grey uniform was there or if khaki still held the place. Every now and then a shower of shrapnel struck the roof of the cottage, and tiles went rattling to the road. All the while a section of our artillery fired incessantly. How gallant those guns of ours sound—Boom-boom-boom. They were fighting to their last shell. If the village went, they went with it. No horses could be brought up to draw them away in such an inferno. The doctor worked on quietly. His work extended now to houses on the left and right. He said it was terrible to see the fear of death on the faces of men shot through the stomach. He found time once to have a cup of tea with me and smoke a cigarette. Night began to fall and the room grew dark. I was glad of his company for five minutes. We were in the same boat, he told me—if the Germans got the village he was going to stay behind with the wounded.

At half-past five Evans came in with a smashed arm.

"Goyle has gone," he said. "He was hit twice before during the day. He was holding out with a few men there and got a third through the chest which did him. Edwards was shot through the knee, and we had to leave him. All the company officers are down. A company has been surrounded and cut off. Whew! you can't live out there." As he spoke the firing swelled to a din unequalled through the day. We heard shouts and curses. The Germans were making a final tremendous effort to break through.

"Our boys may do it," said Evans, "but there are not many left." I lay back against the wall, pulled out a cigarette, and threw one to Evans. We could only wait. Suddenly outside we heard a stamp of feet, a hoarsely yelled order, "Fix bayonets!" another word of command, and a mass of men rushed past the window up the street, cheering madly.

"That's the ——s," cried a stretcher-bearer, who came in excitedly. "They have been sent up from the reserve."

The doctor came in. "We've got two more regiments up; we shall be all right now," he said.

For a moment the firing continued, then died down. Night came and found us still holding the village, and at ten o'clock the ambulance took us away.

XX. "AND THENCE TO BED"

THE horse ambulance took us back some three miles to the field ambulance, where we spent the night after being given some food and tea and having our wounds dressed. The accommodation was rough, just some straw on the floor, but to feel there were three miles between ourselves and the enemy gave one quite a feeling of being rested. At these field ambulances the work of dressing the wounded goes on incessantly day and night, and it is here that many a case of lockjaw or gangrene is prevented by the timely application of antitetanus injection or iodine. Among the wounded was a young German boy, not more than eighteen years old. The other wounded Tommies and the orderlies were very good to him, making quite a pet of the boy and giving him tea and cigarettes and asking him what he thought about the war. He had only had six weeks' training before being sent into the firing-line, and was a gentle enough creature

"AND THENCE TO BED" 221

bewildered by the fierce struggle into which he had been thrown.

In the morning a fleet of motor ambulances came to take us to the clearing hospital at railhead. Most of these ambulances were private cars fitted up at their owners' expense and driven in many cases by the owners too. Only those who have been wounded and travelled in a Government horse ambulance can appreciate the good work done by these volunteer Red Cross workers and their cars. After the lumbering horse vehicle rubber tyres and the well-hung body of a private car are an unspeakable relief to broken bones. Our driver was a young fellow who looked as though he had just left Oxford or Cambridge. He drove us very slowly and carefully over the twelve miles of bumpy road, and took us straight to the station in time to have us put on a hospital train which was leaving that morning for the base. How often at the beginning of the war on my way up to the Front had I seen these hospital trains go by and wondered—with a very pious hope that it might be so—if it would ever be my lot to take a passage in one. In those days as now every one knew that it was only a question of time before they were killed or wounded—few last long enough to become diseased—and to be stowed safely away in a hospital train labelled for England was the best fate that could befall anyone.

It was, then, with a feeling of supreme contentment that I allowed myself to be laid along the seat of a first-class carriage and propped up behind with a greatcoat and a pillow. On the opposite seat was a young gentleman not nearly so contented. He had been hit in the shoulder. He said his wound was hurting him; that he was not comfortable on the seat of the carriage; and that he considered tinned stew (which had just been brought us) a very nasty luncheon. I thought him a peevish and graceless cub and, when he snapped at the orderly who came to clear away lunch, rebuked him.

I said that he ought to be thankful for being where he was at all; that his wound was nothing compared to those of others in the train; that his whining and peevishness brought discredit on his uniform and regiment; and that he ought to be ashamed of himself for making such a fuss. As he was a second lieutenant just fresh from Sandhurst and I was an elderly subaltern of several years' service he did not argue with me, but looked at the floor, while I scowled at him from time to time across the carriage.

Eventually the train started and we began our journey to Boulogne. We had been told it would take about nine hours, and so prepared to make ourselves as comfortable as possible and sleep. Except for a visit from the doctor to ask if we wanted anything, and from a hospital nurse, nothing much happened for the rest of the day. The visit from the hospital nurse is one of the things I remember most clearly from an otherwise clouded period. It was the first taste of the infinite sympathy and solicitude which women give to men returned from the war. All who have experienced it— as every wounded man has in abundant measure —must have felt that anything he has suffered was worth such a reward.

After the visit from the hospital nurse we had some dinner and settled down for the night. About this time I began to notice that the blanket which had been folded in four and placed under my injured leg was slightly rucked at the corner. I could not reach it to adjust it myself and after the scene with my stable mate did not like to ask his assistance. Presently an orderly came by and I called him in to put it right. Half an hour later the same thing happened again and I had to call in another orderly. The little subaltern, who was dozing, opened one eye and looked at me reproachfully, but said nothing. Later, when the train pulled up with a jerk which nearly threw us off our seats, we both groaned softly, and when it did the same thing again I swore, and received a grateful look from the rebuked grumbler. In fact, to shorten the story, by noon the next day, when we were finally taken out of the train, I was half hysterical with pain, discomfort, and fatigue, and the little subaltern had nearly forgotten his troubles in his efforts to adjust my blankets with his sound arm and running to and fro fetching the orderly : the moral of this story needs no pointing. . . .

At Boulogne we were taken by motor ambulance to one of the base hospitals. The hospital was a marvellous example of efficient emergency organization. Three days before it had been a hotel ; and in this space of time —*i.e.* three days—the entire building had been

"AND THENCE TO BED" 225

converted into a thoroughly modern hospital with wards and operating-theatre. Most of the work had been done by the members of the hospital staff themselves, and, as we were taken in, the last bits of hotel furniture were still standing in the hall waiting to be removed.

By this time I was rather exhausted, and I cannot remember more than a matron in a dark silk dress with a very gentle, pretty face bending over me and asking me if I was comfortable, and my replying in a voice that was little above a whisper that it was good to be in bed. I think she said, too, something to the nurse about " not putting him to bed like that." I had been in the same clothes for a fortnight and they were very muddy, and I remember having my breeches cut off and being helped into a flannel night-shirt. I woke later to find a nurse beside me with a basin of water. " Would you like to wash ? " she asked. I gazed at her apathetically. " Come on then, I'll do it for you," she said kindly. She dipped a piece of flannel in the basin and rubbed it gently over my face. Then she took one of my hands and rubbed that ; then streaks of white appeared down my fingers as the caked mud was cleared.

"There, I think that is all we'll do for the present," she said, and feeling beautifully clean —though in reality with ten days' beard and looking perfectly filthy—I lay back on the pillow.

After tea I sat up, accepted a cigarette from my neighbour, and took stock of the rest of the ward.

In the bed on my right was a man with a bandaged head; he had an orderly beside him and was dictating a letter. He was evidently feeling very weak, for he spoke with an obvious effort. The letter was about some lost baggage, and dictated with the utmost precision and detail. He ended by saying, "Signed James Brown, Captain and Adjutant"; and I couldn't help smiling, for it was so like an Adjutant to dictate a precise letter about some lost baggage, but it seemed so funny for him, weakened by his wounds as he was, to be lying there in bed doing it, and I felt sure it was more from force of habit than anything else.

At eight o'clock the day-sister made a round of the wards with the night-sister, handing over her patients till the next day. The night-sister was followed by a sort of understudy who,

I remember, was tall and thin with rather a long nose. This understudy, who was referred to as "nurse" by the other two, was, I gathered, a sort of probationer, and not allowed to take much responsibility on herself.

By ten the ward was in darkness except for one green-shaded light, and I think I must have dozed a little, for I remember looking up suddenly to see the night-sister's understudy standing at the foot of my bed and gazing at me with a puzzled expression. Seeing me open my eyes she stretched out her arm and pulled towards her a glass-topped table with a bowl of dressings on it. Then she studied me again. I was still half asleep and watched her with half-closed eyes.

"Is it your *feet?*" she asked.

I nodded.

She lifted the bedclothes back from the foot of the bed and surveyed my bandaged feet for a minute or two. Then with a sudden air of determination she bent down and, catching my right foot by the big toe, lifted it deftly off the pillow on which it was resting. I gave one piercing scream which woke the whole ward and brought the night-sister running in.

228 WITH MY REGIMENT

For the rest of the night I lay with one eye peeping over the sheet prepared to yell for help at the top of my voice if the young lady assistant came near my bed. The next day she returned to England for further instruction.

The following afternoon I was operated on and the bullet extracted from my ankle. A sergeant brought it me wrapped in cotton-wool and left me feeling quite reassured about the success of the operation. . . .

I remember very well on the way up to the Front seeing a hospital ship leave one of the base ports. She was a beautiful looking vessel, painted white, with a great red cross painted on either side amidships. That hospital ship certainly looked comfortable, and I don't mind admitting that, at the time, I wished most heartily I was on board her with my job done instead of having to go up to the firing-line and do it. The wounded men on board all looked so happy and comfortable.

However, everything comes to him who waits —nothing more quickly than a bullet in these sanguinary days—and after a week at the base hospital at Boulogne I was given a ticket

"AND THENCE TO BED 229

marked " cot case " and told I was going to be put on board a hospital ship for England. I smiled gratefully at the doctor, tied the ticket round my neck, put on a woollen waistcoat, muffler, and dressing-gown (all presented to me by the hospital) over my pyjamas, and waited my turn to be carried downstairs. In due course, with three others, I was taken in a motor ambulance to the ship, and from thenceforward was in the charge of the naval authorities.

We were carried up the gangway on our stretchers and placed on a sort of luggage lift which in the twinkling of an eye transported us below, where we were lifted on to swinging cots arranged in a large saloon. The quick, handy way in which everything was done was typical of the Navy, and having once spent six weeks on board a battleship, I felt quite at home again. Dinner was brought round soon after getting on board, and I ate soup, fish, roast mutton, and apple tart with the heartiest of appetites. Unfortunately, also, in the happiness of the moment, I drank a large bottle of Bass which seriously affected my slumbers during the night.

We did not leave until the following night,

arriving at Plymouth at nine o'clock the next morning. However, it was no hardship to be aboard the hospital ship.

The cots were just as comfortable as beds; there was every appliance for dressing our wounds, and the nurses and doctors looked after us indefatigably. In such surroundings aspects of the war which are taken more seriously elsewhere are made light of. The patients made jokes about each other's wounds and their own, and all were so glad to be alive that pain and suffering were almost forgotten. There was one fellow in the cot next to mine who in the middle of a silence suddenly uttered an exclamation of annoyance. Asked what was the matter, he said he wanted to know the time and had just discovered he had lost his watch. It was a wrist watch, he explained, and must have been left on the arm they had amputated at the field ambulance.

At Plymouth we were taken on board a launch and landed at a quay close by the naval hospital. The ingenious cots devised by the Navy enable a wounded man to be moved bodily in his bed, all wrapped up and warm, to the bed in the hospital. They are so made

"AND THENCE TO BED" 231

that they can either be carried as stretchers, or slung from a ship's side, or put on handtrolleys and wheeled. The Naval Hospital at Plymouth is a model of neatness and smartness, each patient in the officers' quarters gets a small room to himself which is called a cabin; the orderlies are all ex-sailors and handy and obliging as only sailors can be; and the naval nurses in their smart blue uniforms are a pleasure to watch.

I stayed at Plymouth for five days, when I was allowed to travel to London.